Study Guide

for use with
Sociology
An Introduction

Sixth Edition

Richard Gelles
University of Rhode Island

Ann Levine

Prepared by
Kenrick S. Thompson
Arkansas State University, Mountain Home

McGraw-Hill College

Boston   Burr Ridge, IL   Dubuque, IA   Madison, WI   New York   San Francisco   St. Louis
Bangkok   Bogotá   Caracas   Lisbon   London   Madrid
Mexico City   Milan   New Delhi   Seoul   Singapore   Sydney   Taipei   Toronto

McGraw-Hill College

A Division of The McGraw-Hill Companies

Study Guide for use with
SOCIOLOGY: AN INTRODUCTION

1 2 3 4 5 6 7 8 9 0 QPD/QPD 9 3 2 1 0 9 8

ISBN 0-07-024768-4

http://www.mhhe.com

STUDY GUIDE

CONTENTS

CONTENTS, ctnd

INTRODUCTION

This **Study Guide** is designed to accompany Gelles and Levine's SOCIOLOGY: AN INTRODUCTION, **Sixth Edition**. First and foremost, the reader should be aware that this **Study Guide** is not a substitute for reading the chapters in the textbook. Concepts that are defined in the following pages are elaborated upon in the text; research investigations that are cited in this supplement receive detailed treatment in the text. If you read the summaries in the **Study Guide** but omit the text, you are only cheating yourself, and it is likely that your final grade will reflect this "short-cut" strategy.

Here is what the **Study Guide** *can* provide:

- a summary of important concepts, issues, and applications in the chapters you are reading

- a more detailed review of each chapter than the end-of-chapter summaries in the text

- several indicators of how well you have mastered the material in each chapter

- instant feedback on your comprehension of the presentations in each chapter

The **Study Guide** is organized as follows: Each chapter begins with a list of objectives that are phrased as questions and are arranged in the order in which the material is presented in the chapter. These questions parallel the summary sections of each chapter in the text.

Next to appear is a matching exercise based on the boldfaced and/or italicized terms and concepts in the text. These terms should not be viewed as irrelevant jargon to be memorized, but as new ideas which will help you to make sense out of society and social organization.

The chapter review section highlight the main points made in the chapter under consideration. This section provides a much more detailed discussion of the relevant issues than the summaries presented at the conclusion of each chapter in the text. When you check your answers, circle the ones that you missed and then review the definitions using the text and the page citations provided.

The review questions are multiple-choice items based on theories and research findings presented in each chapter of the text. These questions do not necessarily follow the order of topics in the chapters; this "scrambled" organization is designed to reflect the question format that may appear on the examinations in the course you are taking. In the *Answers* section, the correct answer to each question is given, along with a brief explanation. Reference is also made (in parentheses) to the section/subsection in the text where the material is discussed and the relevant page citations. If the answer you select is incorrect, go back and read that section again.

The critical thinking section consists of information and questions designed to show how you can apply sociological concepts and research findings to relevant discussions of social issues and personal concerns. Hopefully, these items will bring some of the issues under examination "to life."

A *Web Exercise* is presented at the conclusion of each chapter in the **Study Guide**. This feature provides you with an opportunity to explore relevant issues using the Internet and World Wide Web and it is hoped that you can have a little fun with the activities presented.

"Doing sociology" can be both rewarding and enjoyable. At the very least, this **Study Guide** should help you to earn a better grade in your introductory sociology course. In addition, perhaps the pages that follow will make your experience that much more satisfying and useful.

Kenrick S. Thompson

PART ONE

INTRODUCING SOCIOLOGY

Chapter One

THE SOCIOLOGICAL PERSPECTIVE

OBJECTIVES

After reading Chapter One, you should be able to provide detailed responses to the following questions:

1. What is sociology?
2. What are the practical uses of sociology?
3. What is the relationship between sociology and common sense?
4. What is the sociological imagination?
5. How does the sociological explanation of suicide differ from commonsense explanations? Why did French sociologist Emile Durkheim reject idiographic explanations in favor of nomothetic ones?
6. What is the difference between conventional wisdom as reflected in the TV news media and what people learn about the "real world" from studying sociology?

CHAPTER REVIEW

Explaining Poverty

The "Rosa Lee" story leaves many questions unanswered involving poverty. What causes poverty? What can be done about it? Public opinion varies on these issues and people tend to give conflicting answers. Overall, however, Americans tend to hold individuals responsible for their own economic circumstances. In the abstract, Americans are sympathetic toward the poor but sense many inconsistencies in government policy. Looking at individuals does not explain the phenomenon of poverty: This is where sociology comes in.

Sociologists examine social forces, looking at trends and overall patterns. To explain social patterns, sociologists draw on the concepts of social structure and culture, among others. Sociologists use what C. Wright Mills called the *sociological imagination*: the ability to see the connection between private troubles (such as Rosa Lee's) and social problems (like urban poverty).

I.   What is Sociology?

Sociology is one division in the family of social sciences that seeks to explain patterns of human behavior. Specifically, sociology is the systematic study of the groups and societies that people create and of how these, in turn, affect the people who create and maintain them.

All social sciences are concerned with human behavior, but although they share the same basic subject matter, each social science focuses on a different aspect of behavior. Your text explains sociology by comparing it to other social sciences, especially psychology. Psychologists are most interested in the internal sources of behavior, in contrast to sociologists, who concentrate on the external sources; psychologists focus on personality, sociologists on social roles. Sociologists are primarily interested in areas where social structure and culture intersect. The most unique feature of sociology is its focus on institutionalized inequality, or "social stratification."

II.   The Challenge of Sociology

Society is changing rapidly.   Perhaps the most immediate task of sociology is to provide a framework for understanding such changes, in both our public affairs and our private lives.

A.   Sociology can make people aware of the different ways in which social arrangements shape their lives. The discipline can enlighten the general public concerning the nature and the effects of such social arrangements.

B.   Sociology permits the user to examine the assumptions underlying conventional wisdom, and to correct popular ideas that are incorrect.

C.   Sociology permits the identification of problems that the public has not yet recognized.

       D.   Sociologists can design and evaluate alternative solutions to social problems. This includes problems in the private sector, as illustrated by William J. Wilson's recommendations concerning social policy on the poverty problem.

       E.   Sociology can help people better understand their own experiences, problems, and prospects. Sociological imagination helps people see that personal failings and personal failures are often the result of *social forces* and permits their personal problems to be seen in perspective.

III.   Sociology and Common Sense

On occasion, sociological findings and common sense do overlap, but often, sociology challenges popular wisdom. Common sense holds that "seeing is believing." Sociologists have found the reverse is also true: What we believe often determines what we see; our perceptions are filtered through the lens of our previous experiences, attitudes, and beliefs. Much of what we know, we know through others. Solomon Asch's experimentation offers dramatic evidence of the impact of groups on individuals and the extent to which reality is based on shared definitions.

IV.   Suicide in Sociological Perspective

Suicide is an act that cries out for explanation. Why did the victim do it? Commonsense explanations and news reports tend to rely on *idiographic explanations*, focusing on why a particular person committed suicide. *Nomothetic explanations*, on the other hand, isolate the key factors associated with all or most suicides in order to help us understand the underlying trends and patterns.

The French sociologist Emile Durkheim's classic study of suicide illustrates this nomothetic approach, thus reflecting the sociological perspective. Durkheim used the sociological method to test the many alternative explanations of suicide that were being debated at the time. By examining all of the relevant variables, Durkheim funneled through the speculation and emerged with a factual explanation: His analysis revealed that variations in suicide rates among different groups could not be explained by mental illness, ethnic or racial background, or climate. He concluded that there was something about the group itself that encouraged or discouraged suicide.

Your text traces Durkheim's intellectual journey to show how he came to identify four different types of suicide:

       A.   Egoistic suicide occurs under conditions of *excessive individualism*, when people have become detached from groups that might have inspired their loyalty and participation.

      B.   Altruistic suicide, in contrast, occurs under conditions of *excessive attachment*, when individuals identify so closely with a group or community that their own lives have no independent value.

      C.   Anomic suicide occurs under conditions of anomie, or "lawlessness" in the broad sense, when traditional values and guidelines for behavior have broken down.

      D.   Fatalistic suicide is likely to occur in societies that exercise a high degree of control over their members' emotions and motivations.

      Note that, in each case, Durkheim explained suicide rates in terms of the characteristics of the groups and communities in which people lived, NOT in terms of psychological or biological factors. He argued that trying to explain patterns of social behavior in terms of individual motives resembles attempting to understand the human body by describing individual cells. Society is more than the sum of its individual members. Durkheim chose suicide as a subject because it illustrates how social forces are social facts, and how these forces influence a form of behavior that most of us consider intensely private. That social forces influence such behavior is a key point in the chapter and one of the basic lessons of sociology.

V.   Sociology and TV News

      Many Americans acquire most of their information about the world from the groups within which they interact, and from the mass media, especially the TV news. What image of the world does the TV news present? How does this image differ from the sociological perspective?

      A.   On television, news items are presented *bite by bite*, with little effort to place them in social or historical context. The viewer learns the *who, what, when, and where*, but seldom the *why*. Sociology is concerned with establishing connections between events, tracing patterns, and thus making sense out of current events.

      B.   The TV news focuses on dramatic events and famous people. What we see on the home screen often seems more real than people's own everyday experience. Events that cannot be portrayed visually receive little attention on TV news. Sociologists are as interested in ordinary people and commonplace events as they are in exceptional people and behavior.

      C.   What famous and important people do and say makes news;

television is particularly well suited to dramatic portrayals of individuals. Further, what famous and important people do and say makes news: the *unique personality*. From the sociological perspective, the cumulative effect of the decisions ordinary people make in their everyday lives may do more to alter the course of history than any particular event or single individual.

      D.   Much of what people see on the TV news is *bad news*: violent crime, natural disasters, and international conflict. Although TV journalists don't deliberately distort the facts, they tend to concentrate on the most sensational ones, thus making the "best stories." Whereas TV news plays on our emotions, sociology encourages people to look more objectively at a wider range of facts.

      E.   TV news is big business and exhibits many of the characteristics of large corporations. The TV news claims to tell us what is happening in our world, but the news media are necessarily selective, tending to support the status quo. Sociology, on the other hand, helps to explain what is selected as "news," how it is packaged, and why. Studying sociology helps people to become active interpreters of the news, not just passive spectators.

CONCEPT REVIEW

Match each of the following terms with the correct definition:

a. social forces (p.8)
b. anomic suicide (p. 28)
c. commonsense impressions of the social world (pp. 19-20)
d. sociological imagination (p. 10)
e. altruistic suicide (p. 26)
f. sociology (p. 10)
g. anomie (p. 28)

h. egoistic suicide (p. 25)
i. fatalistic suicide (p. 28)
j. idiographic explanations (p. 21)
k. nomothetic explanations (p. 23)
l. social stratification (p. 13)
m. social structure (p. 9)
n. culture (p. 10)
o. social institutions (p. 12)

1.___   Suicide that results from lack of attachment to social groups or a community, as opposed to suicide resulting from *too much* of an attachment.

2.___   The variable patterns of individual and collective action and changing attitudes and assumptions that shape our social climate.

3.___   The ability to see the connection between private troubles and social problems.

4.___ A breakdown in the collective social order.

5.___ Suicide that results from a major disruption of the social order.

6.___ The systematic study of the groups and societies in which people live; how social structures and cultures are created and maintained or changed; and how they affect our behavior.

7.___ Suicide that results from excessive attachment to a group or community.

8.___ Often incorrect perceptions, based on the obvious, the mundane, and everyday interaction.

9.___ Occurs in societies that exercise a high degree of control over their members' emotions and motivations.

10.___ Result from the individualized explanation of a single case

11.___ Isolate the relatively few factors associated with phenomena in order to help understand the underlying trends and patterns.

12.___ The social positions, networks of relationships, and institutions that hold a society together and shape people's opportunities and experiences.

13.___ The values, attitudes, habits, and behavioral styles people learn from the community to which they belong.

14.___ The division of society into different layers (or strata) whose occupants have unequal access to social opportunities and rewards, unequal power and influence, and unequal life chances.

15.___ Established patterns of action and thought that organize important social activities-the family, education, religion, the political and economic systems.

Answers

1.	h	6.	f	11.	k
2.	a	7.	e	12.	m
3.	d	8.	c	13.	n
4.	g	9.	i	14.	l
5.	b	10.	j	15.	o

REVIEW QUESTIONS

These questions test your overall grasp of the material in each chapter. The correct answers, with a short explanation, are printed at the end of each section.

1. When pollsters ask why people are poor, Americans tend to:
    a.   give consistent answers
    b.   hold society responsible for the poor's economic circumstances
    c.   be sympathetic toward the poor
    d.   all of the above

2. According to the text's discussion of television news:
    a.   television plays on the common-sense notion that "seeing is believing"
    b.   what we see on TV is readily discernible from the reality of our everyday experience
    c.   television refutes the old saying, "a picture is worth a thousand words"
    d.   events that receive extensive coverage on TV news have less impact than those that cannot be pictured

3. Emile Durkheim was the first sociologist to systematically examine a number of different types of suicide. Which of the following did Durkheim cite as an example of altruistic suicide?
    a.   the high suicide rate in Protestant nations
    b.   the high suicide rate during economic booms
    c.   the high suicide rate among soldiers
    d.   the high suicide rate among single people

4. What we think we see physically can be affected by our interactions with others. This was illustrated by a discussion of which of the following research investigations?
    a.   Solomon Asch's experiments with the effects of group pressure on human perceptions
    b.   Kanter's research with Indsco
    c.   Erikson's study of Buffalo Creek
    d.   Phillips' study of copycat suicides

5. As used in the text, the phrase *bad news bias* refers to:
    a.   the *great man theory* of history
    b.   inaccurate reporting of the facts
    c.   the misrepresentation of white-collar crime
    d.   the over reporting of conflict, hardship, and disasters

6. The text notes that the President of the United States accounts for about 20 percent of all domestic news coverage. This fact illustrates the principle of:
    a.   bad news bias
    b.   news as big business
    c.   news as the unique personality
    d.   news as the dramatic picture

7. The text points out that as a result of centralization, the news tends to be homogenized, with overlapping coverage of the same events, told from similar political viewpoints. This fact illustrates the principle of:
    a.   bad news bias
    b.   news as big business
    c.   news as the unique personality
    d.   news as the dramatic picture

8. The term *sociological imagination* refers to:
    a.   a strategy for reducing wars, unemployment, and divorce
    b.   what sociologists have and nonsociologists lack
    c.   C. Wright Mills's theory of history
    d.   the ability to understand personal problems from a social perspective

9. In their investigations of wife abuse and violence against women in general, the British sociologists Rebecca and Russell Dobash focused on:
    a.   the character disorders of men who battered their wives
    b.   the social characteristics of men who abused their wives
    c.   the patriarchal organization of society that allowed or even required men to control women
    d.   all of the above

10. Durkheim's classic work, *Suicide*, was based on:
    a.   interviews with families of individuals who had committed suicide
    b.   logical analysis of the possible motives for suicide
    c.   systematic analysis of official statistics on suicide
    d.   biological and environmental theories of the day

11. Commonsense and media interpretations of suicide usually rely on:
    a.   idiographic explanations
    b.   nomothetic explanations
    c.   sociological explanations
    d.   absurdity

12. _____ explanations isolate the relatively few factors associated with all or most suicides in order to help us understand the underlying trends and patterns.
    a.   Idiographic
    b.   Nomothetic
    c.   Isometric
    d.   Reflexive

13. Sociologist William J. Wilson has been one of President Clinton's chief advisors on urban poverty and welfare reform. Which of the following is/are among Wilson's recommendations concerning social policy on poverty?
    a.   the elimination of workfare programs
    b.   ensured separation of cities and surrounding suburbs
    c.   national educational standards
    d.   a clear-cut distinction between education and employment

14. The fact that suicide rates are higher for single than for married people, and higher for childless couples than for couples with children, illustrates _____ suicide.
    a.   egoistic
    b.   altruistic
    c.   anomic
    d.   fatalistic

15. In his investigations of *copycat suicides*, sociologist David Phillips found that:
    a.   pre-teenage youngsters are more prone to copycat suicidal behavior than are people of other ages
    b.   copycat suicides take place regardless of how suicide stories are reported in the media
    c.   only among adolescents does the power of media suggestion seem to override the effects of sex and race
    d.   youthful, imitative suicides cannot be prevented

16. In discussing TV news as big business, the text observes that:
    a.   communications industries have been controlled by a handful of corporations since the mid-1960s
    b.   in 1996, between six and ten corporations controlled newspapers, magazines, radio, television, books, and movies
    c.   in 1984, about 15 corporations controlled the communications industries
    d.   none of the above

17. Media analyst Michael Parenti points out that today, the U.S. news media
    a.   are monitored for censorship by a federal body
    b.   are uncensored
    c.   are composed of reporters who have no autonomy whatsoever
    d.   engage in "self-censorship"

18. Which of the following studies might you be likely to find in a sociological journal?
    a.   case histories of individual workers under stress
    b.   an analysis of the effects of family size on student achievement
    c.   a biomedical study of drug dependency
    d.   a discussion of symbolic logic

19. Durkheim argued that variations in the suicide rate must be explained in terms of:
    a.   individual motives
    b.   social forces
    c.   altruism
    d.   egoism

20. The text points out that the main lesson, and message, of sociology is that
    a.   the structure of society affects people's attitudes and behavior
    b.   society overrides all that is psychological within the individual
    c.   all of those who practice sociology must have no personal values whatsoever
    d.   all of the above

Answers

1. c: Polls show that Americans tend to give conflicting answers to the question of why people are poor and they tend to hold individuals responsible for their own economic circumstances. (Explaining Poverty; p. 7)

2. a: What we see on TV often seems more real to people than our own everyday experience, television tends to prove the old saying, "a picture is worth a thousand words, and events that receive extensive coverage on TV news have more impact than those that cannot be pictured. (News as the Dramatic Picture; pp. 29-31; 34-38)

3. c: Altruistic behavior is associated with *excessive loyalty*. The best-known example of this is the tradition of hara-kiri among Japanese soldiers. (Altruistic Suicide; pp. 25-27)

4. a: The subjects of the Asch experiments were given incorrect

answers during the trials by others in the groups (who were research confederates). Most subjects went along with the majority (group) opinion. (The Social Definition of Reality; p. 20)

5. d: The phrase *bad news bias* is used, not to condemn news reporting, but to point out a dramatic flair in broadcasting that may create false impressions. (The Bad-News Bias; pp. 34-35)

6. c: What famous and important people do and say makes news. When it was alleged that President Bill Clinton had engaged in sexual intimacy with a young White House intern, this made national news. (News as the Unique Personality; p. 31)

7. b: Eight corporations own controlling shares in the three major TV networks, forty subsidiary TV stations, and more than 200 cable TV systems, along with other media enterprises. (News as Big Business; pp. 35-37)

8. d: Mills advocated a way of looking at private troubles within a larger perspective, often outside the control of the individual. The sociological imagination allows us to see that personal problems may not be due to an individual failing; there are often social forces at work over which individuals have no control whatsoever. (Sociological Imagination; p. 10)

9. c: Dobash and Dobash used a feminist perspective and focused on the patriarchal organization of society rather than the character disorders of men who battered their wives or the social characteristics of such men. (Identifying Social Problems; pp. 15-16)

10. c: Durkheim's objective was to show that scientific examination of the social facts is more valuable than philosophical, psychological, or any approach(es) which emphasize(s) suicide as an act of individual terms, or speculation. (Durkheim's Sociological Analysis; pp. 24-25)

11. a: Using the idiographic approach, one analyzes the many special circumstances that differentiate a particular event or person from other similar ones. The result is an individualized explanation of a single case. (Suicide in Sociological Perspective; pp. 21-22)

12. b: The word "nomothetic" comes from the Greek *nomo*, which means "law." Research in the physical sciences is based on the nomothetic approach, and Durkheim adopted this strategy in his investigations of suicide. (Suicide in Sociological Perspective; pp. 23-24)

13. c: Wilson made five recommendations: national education standards, linking schools to employers, family support, programs to integrate cities and surrounding suburbs, and genuine workfare. (The Challenge of Sociology: Designing Solutions; pp. 16-17)

14. a: Parents (especially in families with many children) are active participants in a group that commands their loyalty, reducing the chances for suicide. (Egoistic Suicide; p. 25)

15. c: Phillips and his colleagues found that teenagers are more prone to copycat suicides than are people of other ages; that the impact of suicide stories is in part the result of the way they are reported; and that the tragedy is that these youthful, imitative suicides might be prevented, in addition to the fact that only among adolescents does the power of media suggestion seem to override the effects of sex and race. (Sociology and the Media: Copycat Suicides; pp. 32-33)

16. b: Twenty-five years ago, communications media were still separate industries, each dominated by one or a few large companies; today, the number of controlling firms in all of these media has shrunk-- from fifty corporations in 1984 to twenty-three in 1990, to between six and ten in 1996. At the same time, the boundaries between different media have largely disappeared. (Sociology and TV News: TV News as Big Business; pp. 35-37)

17. d: Broadcasters exercise what media analyst Michael Parenti calls "self-censorship"--there are no actual censors checking the news; there is no established body responsible for censorship; and although reporters exercise autonomy, this is done within limits set by those who pay their salaries. (Sociology and TV News: News as Big Business; pp. 35-37)

18. b: Sociologists study the effects of groups on behavior. Case studies are used in psychology; biomedical research is the province of physical science; and logic is a question for philosophers. (What is Sociology?; pp. 10-13)

19. b: Durkheim held that social facts (such as the suicide rate) can only be explained in terms of social forces--in this case, the success or failure of accepted rules and reasons for living in linking people to a community. (Durkheim's Sociological Analysis; 24-25)

20. a: The main lesson, and message, of sociology is that the structure of society affects people's attitudes and behavior; sociologists would never maintain that society completely overrides the individual, and they are well aware that *all* individuals have personal values; sociologists are mandated to *suspend* their values when conducting research. (What Is Sociology?; pp. 10-13)

CRITICAL THINKING

When you have mastered the basic material in this chapter, you are ready to use what you have learned--in conversations about current events or local gossip; in discussions and papers for some of your other courses; in late-night musings about what it all *means*. These questions are designed to exercise your sociological imagination.

1. You are a reporter on a local newspaper and are asked to write a story on the divorce problem. How might you exercise sociological imagination in your story?

2. You are the same reporter, but this time, your assignment is to write an article about *copycat suicide*. How will the sociological imagination assist you in composing an objective assessment of this phenomenon?

WEB EXERCISE: The Controversy Over Physician-Assisted Suicide

The activities of people like Dr. Jack Kevorkian have raised some extremely controversial questions and moral/ethical problems surrounding *physician-assisted suicide*. Kevorkian is a Michigan physician who has made national news through his active participation in supervising suicides by people who have made the conscious decision to die. Suppose you have been tasked with formulating meaningful social policy on this issue. How will you approach this process? The following web sites will provide some food for thought:

http://www.wnet.org/archive/bid/sb-assisted.html

http://www.libertynet.org/libres/advocacy/ndy_links.html

http://web.lwc.edu/administrative/library/suiaudio.html

Chapter Two

SCIENCE AND THEORY IN SOCIOLOGY

OBJECTIVES

After reading Chapter Two, you should be able to provide detailed answers to the following questions:

1.   What is the science of sociology?
2.   How do sociologists conduct research?
3.   What are the leading theoretical orientations in sociology today?
4.   How do sociologists explain society?
5.   How do sociologists explain everyday behavior?
6.   How are theory and research connected?

CHAPTER REVIEW

I.   Sociology as Science

Which is more reliable: a journalist's observations about the insights of a friend who has just gone through a divorce, or a sociological study of the reasons people get divorced? The answer (the sociological investigation) lies in the scientific method. Like all scientists, sociologists follow five basic rules for establishing and explaining facts. Throughout this course, you should keep these principles in mind. These simple steps will also serve you well in other courses that deal with the scientific method.

   A.   Sociology relies on evidence gathered through systematic observation; sociologists demand proof. In everyday conversation, we often rely on hearsay and beliefs because they seem obvious or logical. Scientists are professional skeptics: They demand empirical, or factual, evidence.

   B.   Sociology is concerned with minimizing error and bias. Sociologists use a variety of techniques (e.g., controls, randomization, etc.) in order to minimize bias and error. These strategies must be used religiously in order to be scientific.

C.   Sociology is a public venture. Open discussion and examination of research give sociology a self-correcting mechanism. Conclusions are never taken as final and absolute, but are always open to question, testing, and revision. No theory or finding, however famous, is accepted uncritically.

D.   In everyday discussions, we often use a single, vivid illustration to make a point. But a single case may be the exception to the rule. Sociology is concerned with generalizations. Scientists study particular cases in order to arrive at generalizations.

E.   Sociology seeks to relate facts to one another and to underlying principles in order to produce theory; sociologists pursue not only descriptions, but also explanations. Theory helps sociologists to predict, understand, and explain events.

II.   The Research Procedure

Your text outlines eight steps that all scientists take in their research:

1.   selecting a topic
2.   reviewing the literature
3.   formulating the problem (translating theories or hunches into hypotheses)
4.   creating a research design (choosing a research method, sampling procedure, and measurements)
5.   collecting data
6.   interpreting and analyzing data (uncovering and explaining patterns in the data, confirming, rejecting, or modifying hypotheses)
7.   publishing findings (making methods and results available to others)
8.   replication (another researcher repeating the study, perhaps with modifications)

III.   Doing Sociological Research

The five research methods that sociologists employ most often are: (1) **surveys** (studies that use standardized questionnaires or interviews to collect data on a comparatively large population); (2) **field studies** (direct observation of social behavior in its natural setting); (3) **experiments** (systematic, controlled examinations of cause and effect); (4) **cross-cultural studies** (comparative investigations of beliefs, customs, and behavior among two or more groups of people with different languages and ways of life); and (5) **historical studies** (use of sources from an earlier time, or from an extended time span).

Your text describes five studies involving the issue of family violence, each using a different research design.

A.   *A Survey: Two National Family Violence Surveys.* Richard Gelles and his colleagues chose the survey approach, beginning in the early 1970s with an exploratory study of their students at the University of New Hampshire, followed in 1976 by the First National Family Violence Survey, culminating in 1985 with a second national survey conducted by telephone. The results of the First National Survey indicated that domestic violence was far more widespread than anyone had imagined. Violence, it seemed, was as much a part of family life as love. The findings of the Second National Survey determined that rates of domestic violence were still very high, but that child abuse had *declined* by 47 percent. This finding met with considerable controversy, as many observers were skeptical. There are several possibilities: the Second Survey used different methods, subjects were more likely to report deviant behavior over the phone than in person; people were less willing to report the use of physical force within the family at a later date; or changes in the social climate produced real changes in behavior. Gelles and his colleagues supported this latter view.

The chief advantage of surveys lies in numbers: With a comparatively small investment of time, a researcher can ask thousands of people hundreds of questions. Standardization is the chief weakness of surveys: They often seem to reduce attitudes, beliefs, and experiences to the lowest common denominator.

B.   *A Field Study: Disciplining Children in Public Places.* Sociologist Bruce Brown was curious about social class differences in the way parents discipline children. Brown felt that the findings of previous investigations were open to distortion because subjects sought to present themselves in a socially desirable light: In their daily interactions with children, are working-class parents as authoritarian, and middle-class parents as reasonable as they claim? Brown conducted a field study to find out: He studied parent-child interaction in shopping malls. Brown found that working-class parents were slightly more likely than middle-class parents to use restrictive disciplinary techniques, but the difference was not statistically significant.

Fieldwork is particularly well suited for making observations, discovering regularities, and generating new ideas; it is the only way to study people in their natural settings. Weaknesses include the possibility of atypical findings, greater subjectivity than other methods, difficulty in generalizing and replicating, problems that relate to the presence of the researchers, and the need for tighter controls.

C.   *An Experiment: The Minneapolis Police Experiment.* Sociologists Lawrence Sherman and Richard Berk designed a field experiment to research the question, "Does arrest act as a deterrent to wife abuse?" Sherman and Berk adapted the experimental method for a study of actual cases of domestic violence. Using a random assignment technique, the researchers compared spouses who had been arrested for domestic violence with those who had no record. They found small but significant differences between the experimental and control groups, leading them to conclude that arrest intervention did not make things worse and may well have made things better. Other studies have determined that arrest works better in some cases of family violence than in others.

The chief advantage of experiments is control; on the negative side, most social experiments are conducted in laboratories; experiments are most useful for studying limited, clearly defined questions.

D.   *A Cross-Cultural Study: Wife Abuse and Modernization in Papua New Guinea.* British sociologist Rebecca Morley set out to discover whether domestic violence is more common in modern, industrialized nations or in traditional, developing countries. Morley and her colleagues used the survey method for cross-cultural purposes. Contrary to what she expected, Morley found that rates of wife beating in urban Papua New Guinea are twice as high as in industrialized nations.

The main advantage of cross-cultural studies is that they enable researchers to identify cultural universals, and they can help to reduce ethnocentrism. The main problem in cross-cultural research is definitions: One cannot assume that the same behavior means the same thing to people in other cultures, and there is always a risk that the researchers themselves will take an ethnocentric view of the society under investigation.

E.   *A Historical Study: The Roots of Violence Against Wives.* Sociologists R. Emerson Dobash and Russell Dobash set out to answer the question of whether families were happier in the past than they are today. They did this by reviewing sources from earlier times, seeking to determine when and why cultural attitudes and social behaviors developed and how they have changed over time. Dobash and Dobash concluded that violence against wives is an extension of patriarchy, and that women's position in early Christian society was not very positive. Not until the late nineteenth century, in the United States and Great Britain, were laws passed banning the use of "excessive" physical force against wives. Although much has changed, Dobash and Dobash determined that old patriarchal attitudes linger.

The advantages of historical studies are similar to those of cross-cultural studies, but they are not as precise as surveys or experiments, nor as rich in detail and emotion as field studies.

Other research techniques include *in-depth interviews, content analysis, and simulation.*

IV.   The Role of Theory

Without theory, science would be a random collection of meaningless facts. Theories enable sociologists to generate relevant questions and findings, guide research, and then organize the results in a meaningful and coherent fashion.

A *theory* is a summary of existing knowledge that provides guidelines for conducting research and interpreting new information. Theories are composed of three basic elements: assumptions, concepts, and propositions. There are three different levels of theory: hypotheses, theories of the middle range, and theoretical orientations.

V.   Explaining Society and Everyday Social Behavior

There are several main theoretical orientations in sociology today. Your text explains these theories.

A.   The *functionalist perspective* is based on the view that societies are made up of specialized structures (the family, religion, economy, politics, education, etc.) and that each of these structures performs a vital function in maintaining the whole. These specialized structures are interdependent. Under normal conditions, they work together to promote harmony and stability. Functionalists emphasize the importance of consensus among members of a society and the potentially harmful effects of sudden change on groups or society. Functionalism has been criticized for supporting the status quo.

Functionalists hold that in order to understand why a behavior pattern exists in a society, one must examine the consequences of that pattern; this may be done by analyzing the latent (unintended) functions as well as the manifest (intended) functions.

B.   *Conflict theory* is based on the view that the structure of society is the result of competition for scarce resources. Marx held that capitalism divides society into two opposing classes: those who control capital/own the means of production and those who must sell their labor. Contemporary conflict theorists have broadened this scenario to account for the cross-cutting interests of diverse groups in society today and for the emergence of a world capitalist system.

Conflict theorists maintain that in order to understand why a behavior pattern exists in society, one must determine who benefits from that pattern and how such persons maintain their positions of power. Some key concepts for conflict sociologists are *power, privilege, prestige, conflict* and *competition.*

VI.　Explaining Everyday Social Behavior

A.　*Symbolic interactionism* focuses on the cumulative effects of individual actions and interpersonal relationships in everyday behavior. This theoretical perspective is premised on the principle that everyday interaction is determined by the way people interpret events and relationships. The emphasis is on the symbolic meanings that people attach to social encounters.

Whereas functionalists and conflict theorists focus on the roles a society creates for people and how that society distributes people among those roles, symbolic interactionists focus on the ways in which people interpret their roles.

Some symbolic interactionists draw an analogy between social life and the theater, in what is called the *dramaturgical approach*. Another branch of symbolic interactionism, *ethnomethodology*, focuses not on the roles people consciously play, but on the routine, mundane behavior that people take for granted. Another area of much interest to symbolic interactionists is *sociolinguistics*. One new area of interest is *social coordination theory*: the effort to establish general principles to explain how social actors coordinate their activities. Key concepts for symbolic interactionists include *meanings, symbols, interaction, self* and *role*.

VII.　The Interplay of Theory and Research

Theory and research are connected through what might be called a "research cycle." Theories generate hypotheses; hypotheses guide researchers in the collection of data; analysis of data yields empirical generalizations; these generalizations may support existing theories or generate new or revised theories; replication leads to further support or revision; this leads to new hypotheses, and so on. In sociology, as in other sciences, the cycle is continuous; the work is never complete, as new findings emerge.

CONCEPT REVIEW

Match each of the following terms with the correct definition.

a.   sample (p. 47)
b.   manifest function (p. 69)
c.   field study (p. 52)
d.   ethnography (p. 57)
e.   experiment (p. 54)
f.   control group (p. 55)
g.   historical study (p. 60)
h.   dependent variable (p. 46)
i.   experimental group (p. 55)
j.   independent variable (p. 46)
k.   scientific proposition (p. 66)
l.   hypothesis (p. 46)
m.   ethnocentrism (p. 60)
n.   representative sampling (p. 47)
o.   sociological concepts (p. 63)
p.   random assignment (p. 55)
q.   theoretical orientations (p. 67)

r.   survey (p. 48)
s.   latent function (pp. 69-70)
t.   theory (p. 63)
u.   cross-cultural study (p. 57)
v.   cultural universals (p. 60)
w.   theory of the middle range (p. 67)
x.   participant observation (p. 52)
y.   theoretical assumption (p. 3)
z.   replication (p. 48)
aa.   science (p. 43)
bb.   conflict perspective (p. 70)
cc.   symbolic interactionism (p. 72)
dd.   functionalist perspective (p. 68)

1.____   A systematic, controlled examination of cause and effect.
2.____   The unintended, and often unrecognized, consequence of a behavior pattern or social arrangement.
3.____   General notions that apply to a number of individual cases; abstract ideas that identify similarities between otherwise diverse social phenomena.
4.____   An extended participant-observer field study during which the researcher lives with or relates closely to the people he or she is studying.
5.____   A testable statement about the nature of a phenomenon.
6.____   The subjects in an experiment who are exposed to all of the experimental conditions *except* the experimental treatment.
7.____   The subjects in an experiment who are exposed to the experimental

treatment, as opposed to a group which is not.

8.___ The intended and recognized consequence of a behavior pattern or social arrangement.

9.___ A research technique in which each member of the population being studied has an equal chance of being selected for investigation.

10.___ The random division of subjects into control and experimental groups.

11.___ A research method involving the use of standardized questionnaires, interviews, or both, to gather data on a large population.

12.___ A summary of existing knowledge that provides guidelines for conducting research and interpreting new information.

13.___ The phenomenon that is treated as an effect or result.

14.___ A research method involving direct, systematic observation of social behavior in its natural setting.

15.___ The belief that one's own culture is superior to that of other people.

16.___ That portion of the population under investigation that the researcher actually studies.

17.___ A broad, general theory that attempts to explain all (or at least the most important) aspects of social life.

18.___ A comparative study of beliefs, customs, and/or behavior among two or more groups of people with different languages and ways of life.

19.___ Statements about the nature of a concept or about the relationship between two or more concepts.

20.___ A review of sources from earlier times that seeks to determine when and why cultural attitudes and social behavior developed and how they have changed over time.

21.___ The factor that is considered a potential cause.

22.___ Values, norms, beliefs, or practices that are found in all cultures.

23.___ Repeating the study with another group of subjects at another place and time, perhaps with modifications in the methods.

24.___ Modest theories, limited in scope and generality and close to the empirical data, that apply to an array of topics, not just one subject.

25.___ Untested notions about the nature of human behavior or social systems.

26.___ A research method where the investigators introduce themselves to their subjects and spend many hours either observing behavior from the sidelines or participating in social activities and conducting in-depth interviews with their subjects.

27.___ Assumes that society is a stable, well integrated, self-regulating *system* that endures because it serves people's basic needs.

28.___ A set of agreed-upon procedures for establishing and explaining facts.
29.___ Assumes that human behavior is determined not by the objective facts of a situation but by the *meanings* people ascribe to a situation.
30.___ Assumes that society is a collection of *competing* interest groups, each with its own goals and agendas.

Answers

1.	e	7.	i	13.	h	19.	k	25.	y
2.	s	8.	b	14.	c	20.	g	26.	x
3.	o	9.	n	15.	m	21.	j	27.	dd
4.	d	10.	p	16.	a	22.	v	28.	aa
5.	l	11.	r	17.	q	23.	z	29.	cc
6.	f	12.	t	18.	u	24.	w	30.	bb

REVIEW QUESTIONS

1. Which of the following reflects a key difference between sociology and the physical sciences?
    a. In sociology, theory and research are linked in a continuous cycle.
    b. When sociologists study individual cases and specific events, they are looking for evidence of general principles.
    c. Research findings are never taken as *the first word* in sociology, but are always open to question.
    d. The subjects of sociological studies may intentionally or unintentionally deceive a researcher.

2. The view that modern societies are divided into many competing groups whose interests crisscross one another, preventing a division into hostile camps, is associated with which of the following schools of thought?
    a. structural functionalism
    b. modern conflict theory
    c. symbolic interactionism
    d. developmentalism

3. The experimental method is often the preference of sociologists. The main advantage of the experimental method is:
    a. flexibility
    b. economy
    c. control
    d. depth

4. Assume that a researcher wants to know whether the average American college student thinks alcohol, marijuana, and nicotine are dangerous drugs. The best investigative strategy would be to:
    a. conduct an experiment
    b. design a survey
    c. carry out a field study
    d. conduct a historical study

5. Modest theories, limited in scope and generality, close to the empirical data, and which apply to an array of topics are termed:
    a. theories of the middle range
    b. hypotheses
    c. scientific propositions
    d. theoretical orientations

6. A team of researchers is conducting an experiment on the effects of TV violence on children's behavior. They show children in Group A a typical cops and robbers program with ten violent con- frontations, and they show children in Group B a film about a sailing crew. They then observe the youngsters in a playground. The children in Group A represent the:
    a. dependent variable
    b. independent variable
    c. control group
    d. experimental group

7. Once a sociologist has selected a research topic and surveyed the literature, the next step is:
   a. choosing a research design
   b. formulating hypotheses
   c. collecting data
   d. analyzing data

8. In their investigations of the history of family violence, Dobash and Dobash concluded that:
   a. women's position in early Christian society was much better than it is today
   b. laws banning the use of "excessive" physical force against wives were passed in the early eighteenth century
   c. violence against wives is an extension of a matrifocal society
   d. violence against wives is an extension of patriarchy

9. In their field experiment involving actual cases of domestic violence in Minneapolis, Lawrence Sherman and Richard Berk:
   a. did not use experimental and control groups
   b. employed the technique of random assignment
   c. found no differences between spouses who had prior arrests for domestic violence and those who did not
   d. concluded that arrest intervention made everything "much worse"

10. Which of the following is a latent function of the U.S. educational system?
    a. providing a baby-sitter
    b. teaching students skills, values, and attitudes
    c. awarding students credentials that they can use as bargaining chips in the job market
    d. teaching young people to follow rules

11. One disadvantage of the survey as a research tool is:
    a. reliance on self-reports
    b. limited scope
    c. the observer effect
    d. flexibility

12.   The main advantage of cross-cultural studies is that they:
   a.   completely eliminate bias
   b.   rule out ethnocentrism
   c.   avoid any problems with definitions
   d.   enable researchers to identify cultural universals

13.   Of the five research methods described in this chapter, which is the most subjective (the most dependent on the researcher's impressions)?
   a.   experiment
   b.   survey
   c.   field study
   d.   historical study

14.   Which of the following statements about the science of sociology is FALSE?
   a.   Sociology is an empirical science.
   b.   Hunches and speculation have no role in sociology.
   c.   Sociologists are concerned with techniques for minimizing bias and error.
   d.   Sociology is a public venture.

15.   The view that society is held together by consensus and interdependence is associated with which of the following theoretical orientations?
   a.   functionalism
   b.   conflict theory
   c.   symbolic interactionism
   d.   ethnomethodology

16.   Professor Jones theorizes that there has been a revolution in perceptions of sexual activity in the past twenty-five years, but comparatively little change in behavior. She decided to test this theory by asking college women how sexually active they think their mothers' generation was before marriage and how many partners they think other women their own age have had before marriage. At what point in the research cycle is Professor Jones now?
   a.   theory building
   b.   construction of hypotheses
   c.   data collection
   d.   empirical generalizations/data analysis

17.   The basic question asked by symbolic interactionists is:
   a.   What are the consequences of a social pattern?
   b.   Who benefits from a social arrangement?
   c.   How are the different elements of society integrated?
   d.   How does everyday behavior support or modify social definitions of reality?

18.   "Society is a collection of competing interest groups, each with its own goals and agendas." This is the main assumption underlying:
   a.   functionalism
   b.   symbolic interactionism
   c.   conflict theory
   d.   ethnomethodology

19.   A researcher wishing to study patterns of divorce rates in the nineteenth century uses court statistics, searches archival records, examines novels, and examines divorce laws as they have come into existence. This is an example of:
   a.   an experiment
   b.   a survey
   c.   a historical study
   d.   a cross-cultural study

20.　　　According to the text, theory and research:
　　　a.　　are interrelated; one could not exist without the other
　　　b.　　are mutually exclusive
　　　c.　　are usually at odds with each other
　　　d.　　are supportive in the absence of hypotheses

Answers

1.　　d:　　All of the other answers apply to the physical as well as the social sciences. (Sociology as Science; p. 43)

2.　　b:　　This view is most closely associated with the contemporary conflict theorist Lewis Coser, whose work can be seen as a revision of Marxist theory in light of the conditions in society today. (The Role of Theory; pp. 71-72)

3.　　c:　　An experiment that includes control groups is the best technique for isolating, and hence controlling, variables. (The Strengths and Weaknesses of Experiments; p. 56)

4.　　b:　　When a researcher is interested in making generalizations about a large population, a survey is most appropriate. (The Strengths and Weaknesses of Surveys; pp. 51-52)

5.　　a:　　There are different levels of theory: Hypotheses are limited, testable propositions; theoretical orientations are broad, general theories that attempt to explain all or the most important aspects of social life; scientific propositions are statements about the nature of a concept or about the relationship between two or more concepts. (The Role of Theory; pp. 66-67)

6.　　d:　　In this experiment, exposure to TV violence is the experimental treatment; the children in Group A are the experimental group; those in Group B are the controls. (The Research Procedure; p. 46)

7.　　b:　　This step in the research procedure involves translating hunches into testable statements about cause and effect. (The Research Procedure; pp. 45-56)

8.　　d.　　Dobash and Dobash found that violence against wives related to ancient customs and laws designed to give men domination and control over women. (Doing Sociological Research; pp. 60-62)

9.　　b:　　Sherman and Berk employed an experimental/control group design, ultimately discovering small, but significant differences between these groups; they concluded that "arrest intervention certainly did not make things worse and may well have made things better."   The researchers employed *random assignment* of people to the experimental and control groups in order to avoid bias. (Doing Sociological Research; pp. 54-56)

10.   a: A person who declared that schools were little more than expensive baby-sitting services would be considered a cynic. Answers b-d describe manifest functions. (Explaining Society: The Functionalist and Conflict Perspectives; pp. 69-70)

11.   a: Participants in a survey may tell a researcher what they think he or she wants to hear. The same is true in interviews conducted as part of field studies, but the latter method allows the researcher to compare people's self-reports with actual behavior. (The Research Procedure; pp. 51-52)

12.   d.   No research design completely eliminates bias, and even though cross-cultural research does help to reduce ethnocentrism, it can't rule it out; the main problem in cross-cultural research is definitions. (The Strengths and Weaknesses of Cross-Cultural Studies; p. 60)

13.   c: Whereas a survey turns respondents' answers into quantifiable data and an experiment has built-in controls, a field study depends on the researcher's observations and relationships with subjects. This is why it is most useful for exploratory research. (The Research Procedure; p. 53)

14.   b: Sociologists do demand empirical evidence.   Nevertheless, imagination (often in the form of speculation and hunches) plays a role in the early stages of research. (Sociology as Science; pp. 42-43)

15.   a: Where traditional functionalists stressed the need for harmony in a society, contemporary functionalists emphasize the delicate balance among different groups in a society. (Explaining Society: The Functionalist and Conflict Perspectives; pp. 68-69)

16.   b: Professor Jones is translating her *theory* into testable statements. She hypothesizes that if the main change is in perceptions and not sexual activity, young women will believe that their mothers' generation was less active than they are, but that other women their own age are more active than they are. (The Research Procedure; p. 46)

17.   d: Answers a and c are the main concerns of functionalists; answer b is the main concern of conflict theorists. (Explaining Society: The Functionalist and Conflict Perspectives; pp. 68-72)

18.   c: Conflict theorists argue that what holds a society together is not consensus, but constraint. Clearly, some groups benefit more from existing social arrangements than others do. (Explaining Society: The Conflict Perspective; pp. 70-72)

19.   c: The aim of a historical study is to research a past event, and/or an event over time. The research has to rely on information gathered by others, or reported in books, newspapers, archives, etc. (A Historical Study: The Roots of Violence Against Wives; pp. 60-61)

20.   a: Scientific theories are firmly grounded in research; theory guides research, and research informs theory. (The Interplay of Theory and Research; p. 74)

CRITICAL THINKING

1.   Your sociology instructor sets up a debate on education. One debating team will be assigned the functional point of view; a second team, conflict theory; a third team, symbolic interactionism. Each team will be asked to explain the GPA perspective among college students. Which team will you join? Why?

2.   A team of sociologists is conducting a field study, similar to that described in the text, on your campus. One of the researchers approaches you in the student lounge, explains the study, and asks for an hour interview. You agree. It is an intensive interview: She asks about your parents' expectations, whether you consider yourself a dedicated student, how you think your friends see you, and countless other questions. Would you answer truthfully?

       Next, suppose you are called into the Dean's office, introduced to a researcher, and asked to participate in the study. Would you agree? Would you give the same answers you gave under the first procedure? What does this tell you about field studies?

       Now imagine that one year later you learn that the *real* purpose of the study was to determine whether extracurricular activities interfere with school performance. You were chosen to participate because you were the captain of the basketball team, or an editor on the school paper, or the leader of an anti-nuclear protest. How would you feel about the study now?

WEB EXERCISE: "The Sociology Corner" on the Internet

The following web site will provide hours of interesting exploration for students who wish to indulge themselves:

http://www.sociology.net/search/search.html

This is the address for "The Sociology Corner," which provides a potpourri of activities for the cyberspace visitor. The site is menu-driven in a fashion that is easy to follow. Pick a topic or two and explore at your leisure. For example, you might want to use the Search Engine to learn more about "theory" or "research methods."

PART TWO

THE DYNAMICS OF
SOCIAL BEHAVIOR

Chapter Three

CULTURE

OBJECTIVES

After reading Chapter Three, you should be able to provide detailed responses to the following questions:

1. Why is the study of culture important?
2. What are the basic elements of culture?
3. How do human beings view the differences among cultures (ethnocentrism, cultural relativism)?
4. How do people improvise within their own culture?
5. How do social scientists explain cultural variations?
6. How and why do cultures change?

CHAPTER REVIEW

I. Culture: An Overview

Culture is a design for living: the shared understandings that people use to coordinate their activities. Human beings *learn* to be human through the socialization process: the ongoing process of interaction through which we acquire a personal identity and social skills. The content of socialization varies from one society to another, and these differences reflect the content of culture. In everyday conversation, *culture* refers to an appreciation of the finer things in life. Social scientists use the term to describe a people's entire design for living.

Much of what we take for granted, as part of *human nature*, is actually the result of enculturation: immersion in a culture to the point where that particular design for living seems "only natural."

II.   What are the basic elements of culture?

Although the contents differ, all cultures consist of six basic elements: beliefs, values, norms and sanctions, symbols, language, and technology. Your text uses examples from American and Vietnamese culture, to illustrate these concepts.

A.   All cultures are grounded in a set of *beliefs*, or shared knowledge and ideas about the nature of life. Whereas Americans think of time as marching on (you can't go back again), the Vietnamese conceive of time in cycles (things come around again).

B.   All cultures set *values*, or shared standards for what is right and desirable. The Vietnamese value family loyalty, adaptability, and propriety. In contrast, Americans value individualism, sticking to one's principles, and assertiveness.

C.   *Norms* translate beliefs and values into specific rules for behavior: the *Thou shalts* and the *Thou shalt nots*. Traditionally, young Vietnamese females are not allowed to leave their homes without a chaperone; their parents have arranged their marriages. In contrast, young American females are expected to date when they reach adolescence; parents advise, but are not supposed to dictate their choice of husband. Norms vary in intensity from sacred taboos to everyday habits (folkways). Norms also vary according to the actor and the situation. Sanctions are the punishments and rewards that people use to enforce norms. Formal sanctions are official public rewards and punishments; informal sanctions are unofficial, sometimes subtle or even unconscious checks on everyday behavior.

D.   *Symbols* are designs or objects that have acquired special cultural meaning. The same object may symbolize different feelings in different cultures. For example, both Americans and Vietnamese bury their dead in coffins, and both may invest a great deal of money in these containers. But traditionally, those Vietnamese who could afford to do so purchased a coffin long before an elderly person died and put it on display -- much to that person's delight. Vietnamese people have "death days," honoring the dead, in much the same fashion that Americans celebrate "birthdays." The most important set of cultural symbols is language.

E.   *Language* is a key element of culture. Whereas other animals communicate via signs (sounds and gestures whose meaning is fixed), humans communicate by means of symbols (sounds and gestures whose meaning depends upon shared understandings). Words can be combined in different ways to convey an unlimited number of messages, not only about the here and now, but also about the past and future, to symbolize that which is absent, and to permit one to examine the impossible as well. Whereas English provides only one term for addressing another person (*you*), Vietnamese provides numerous terms indicating degrees of respect (and illustrating their concern with propriety). According to the *Sapir-Whorf hypothesis*, language causes people to pay attention to certain things, but ignore others. But at the same time, there is little evidence that language determines the way people think, since it is only one element of culture.

F.   *Technology* sets the tone for culture, influencing not only how people work, but also how they socialize and think about the world. Despite global marketing, significant differences in the material environment remain. To rural Vietnamese immigrants, the United Staates may seem as fantastic as Disneyland appears to be among American children.

III.   What is the difference between ethnocentrism and cultural relativity?

Even anthropologists experience culture shock in unfamiliar cultural settings. It is not easy to transplant oneself into another cultural setting and feel comfortable all at once. In fact, adjustment takes a great deal of time and patience. One reason for this lies in an understanding of the term *ethnocentrism*. Most, if not all, peoples have feelings of cultural superiority; they have a high opinion of their own design for living, compared with those of other peoples. Our own culture becomes so much a part of us that we think of our own way of doing things as the only way. Taken out of context, any custom seems peculiar. Your text illustrates this through the "body ritual of the *Nacirema*"--American spelled backward). *Cultural relativity* refers to the view that behavior must be understood in terms of its own cultural context, which is the opposite of ethnocentrism.

IV.   Cultural inconsistencies and diversities

Cultures vary widely in their degree of *cultural integration*--the extent to which different parts of culture fit well together and support one another. Internal inconsistencies and diversities are most visible in large, heterogeneous societies like the United States, but people everywhere devote considerable thought and energy to evading the rules.

Ideal culture consists of norms and values to which people openly and formally adhere; *real culture* consists of norms and values that people may not openly or formally admit to, but practice nonetheless. The interplay between ideal and real culture can result in obvious contradictions. Real culture may be said to consist of *patterned evasions* of the ideal culture.

A *subculture* exists when a group of people has developed a set of variations on cultural norms and values that set these people apart from other members of their society. Subcultures may develop around ethnic identity, occupation, special interests, or even sexual preferences. When a group opposes a number of widely held norms and values, it is known as a *counterculture*. The text discusses the militia movement as an example of a counterculture

V.   Explaining culture

In recent years, attempts to explain both the role that culture plays in society and the relationship between individuals and culture have moved to the forefront of sociology.

Functionalists view culture as a highly integrated system, each element of which contributes something to the whole. In analyzing cultures, they focus on the ways in which beliefs and practices function to satisfy basic human needs and to reinforce commitment to a social system. Put another way, functionalists examine the social consequences of different elements of culture. One group of contemporary functionalist sociologists and anthropologists--called *cultural ecologists*--focuses on the role of the environment in shaping cultures. The text cites Marvin Harris's explanation of the sacred cow in India as a classic example of the cultural ecology approach.

Unlike functionalists, who emphasize the role of culture in promoting social solidarity and adaptation to the environment, *conflict theorists* emphasize the role of culture in the struggle for power and privilege. According to this view, the dominant culture in a society usually benefits some groups at the expense of others. Culture may enhance the power of the elite in some situations, while providing a springboard for revolutionary change in others.

Where does the individual fit in the cultural framework? Most sociologists feel that culture shapes us but that we also shape culture. On the one hand, culture can be seen as the background against which the social drama is played; on the other hand, culture can be seen not as background, but as a product of social behavior. Some sociologists study the production of culture, emphasizing the impact of technology, social structure, and economics; for them, the production of culture is always a collective, social process, not the work of single individuals.

VI.   Cultural change

No culture is static. There are three main sources of large-scale cultural change: alteration in the *natural environment*; *cultural contact* between groups whose norms, values, and technology are different; and *discovery* and *invention*. Cultural change often occurs in fits and starts; there is often a *cultural lag*, or delay between a change in technology (material culture) and changes in beliefs and values (beliefs and values). People require adjustment to change; when changes are dramatic, adjustment can be extremely difficult. Even when change is peaceful and welcome, adjusting to a new design for living is problematic. The text discusses the recent history of the People's Republic of China as a vivid illustration of planned cultural change enforced by the state and unplanned cultural change in response to cultural contact.

CONCEPT REVIEW

Match each of the following terms with the correct definition.

a.	folkways (p. 90)	m.	ideal culture (p. 97)
b.	beliefs (p. 87)	n.	enculturation (p. 85)
c.	sanctions (p. 91)	o.	culture shock (p. 95)
d.	ethnocentrism (p. 95)	p.	socialization (p. 85)
e.	formal sanctions (p. 91)	q.	real culture (p. 97)
f.	language (p. 92)	r.	cultural relativism (p. 96)
g.	subculture (p. 101)	s.	law (p. 90)
h.	counterculture (p. 101)	t.	culture (p. 84)
i.	Sapir-Whorf hypothesis (p. 93)	u.	mores (p. 90)
		v.	technology (p. 93)
j.	values (p. 88)	w.	cultural integration (p. 97)
k.	cultural lag (p. 109)	x.	informal sanctions (p. 91)
l.	symbol (p. 91)	y.	norms (p. 90)

1.___ Shared ideas about how the world operates.
2.___ The view that a culture must be understood in terms of its own meanings.
3.___ The tendency to judge other cultures in terms of one's own and to conclude that the other cultures are inferior.
4.___ Official, public rewards and punishments.
5.___ Norms that are so sacred that violation is unthinkable.
6.___ The socially imposed rewards and punishments that are used to encourage conformity to cultural norms.
7.___ A set of understandings, behaviors, practical and symbolic objects, and vocabulary that distinguish a particular group from other members of their society.
8.___ Broad, abstract, shared standards of what is right, desirable, and worthy of respect.
9.___ Something (e.g., an object) that evokes meaning.
10.___ The ongoing process of interaction through which we acquire a personal identity and social skills.
11.___ Norms and values to which people openly and formally adhere.
12.___ A subculture that actively opposes the values and practices of the larger society.

13.___ The feelings of disorientation and stress that people experience when they enter an unfamiliar cultural setting.

14.___ Norms that are not sacred but are so ingrained that people conform to them automatically, out of habit, in everyday interaction.

15.___ A norm that has been established as a formal code by officials of the state.

16.___ A delay between a change in technology and changes in beliefs and values.

17.___ The idea that our language causes us to pay attention to certain things and to ignore others.

18.___ Norms and values that people may not formally admit to, but practice nonetheless.

19.___ Immersion in a culture to the point where that particular design for living seems *only natural*.

20.___ A people's design for living.

21.___ A set of shared symbols and rules for combining symbols in meaningful ways.

22.___ A body of practical knowledge and equipment for enhancing the effectiveness of human labor and altering the environment for human use.

23.___ The extent to which different parts of culture fit well together and support one another.

24.___ Unofficial, sometimes subtle or even unconscious checks on everyday behavior.

25.___ Rules about what people should or should not do, say, or think in a given situation.

Answers

1.	b	9.	l	17.	i	25.	y
2.	r	10.	p	18.	q		
3.	d	11.	m	19.	n		
4.	e	12.	h	20.	t		
5.	u	13.	o	21.	f		
6.	c	14.	a	22.	v		
7.	g	15.	s	23.	w		
8.	j	16.	k	24.	x		

REVIEW QUESTIONS

1.   A major difference between human cultures and other animals' *designs for living* is that culture:
   a.   is based on instincts
   b.   is a form of adaptation
   c.   is transmitted through learning
   d.   depends on communication

2.   Which of the following is NOT one of the elements of culture identified in the text?
   a.   beliefs
   b.   norms and sanctions
   c.   technology
   d.   deviant behavior

3.   Which of the following is a core value in Vietnamese culture?
   a.   reckoning time in sixty-year cycles
   b.   the notion that family honor is more important than individual goals or even moral principles
   c.   the notion that one should stick to one's principles
   d.   the celebration of death days

4.   The text includes a discussion of genital mutilation in Africa and the Arab peninsula. Most Americans would condemn this practice, but this does not mean that they cannot seek to understand it. This is an example of:
   a.   positive sanctions
   b.   negative sanctions
   c.   ethnocentrism
   d.   cultural relativism

5.   Countless popular songs tell Americans that for every person there is one, and only one, true love. This is an example of:
   a.   real culture
   b.   ideal culture
   c.   subculture
   d.   patterned evasion

6.   The rise of specialized organizations of social control, such as the courts and the police, illustrates the increase in:
   a.   informal sanctions
   b.   informal positive sanctions
   c.   formal sanctions
   d.   informal negative sanctions

7.   A crucifix, a statue of Buddha, a teddy bear, and a constitution are all examples of:
   a.   norms
   b.   symbols
   c.   language
   d.   subcultures

8.   Which of the following is a value?
   a.   Students should not throw spitballs during class.
   b.   Students who cheat on examinations should be suspended.
   c.   All young people have a right to an education.
   d.   College professors should not date their students.

9.   In the not-too-distant past, the Bureau of Indian Affairs created boarding schools for Native American children. The idea was to help youngsters enter the mainstream of U.S. society by separating them from their past and from other members of their tribes. This policy was an example of:
   a.   positive sanctions
   b.   negative sanctions
   c.   ethnocentrism
   d.   cultural relativism

10. The difference between values and norms is that:
    a. values are shared
    b. norms are shared
    c. values apply to specific situations
    d. norms apply to specific situations

11. The notion that men are stronger than women is a:
    a. belief
    b. norm
    c. value
    d. sanction

12. Which theoretical view regards culture as part of an integrated whole?
    a. conflict
    b. functionalist
    c. interactionist
    d. ethnomethodology

13. _____ theorists emphasize the role of culture in the struggle for power and privilege.
    a. Functionalist
    b. Interactionist
    c. Conflict
    d. Developmental

14. According to the Sapir-Whorf hypothesis, language:
    a. shapes our perceptions and thoughts
    b. is the storehouse of culture
    c. is a set of shared symbols
    d. enables people to transmit culture from generation to generation

15.   Which of the following is NOT a type of norm?
      a.   folkways
      b.   mores
      c.   laws
      d.   values

16.   Americans believe that it is wrong to take another human life, yet many Americans support the death penalty. This exemplifies:
      a.   real culture
      b.   ideal culture
      c.   the contradiction between ideal and real culture
      d.   patterned evasion

17.   The rule about putting your napkin in your lap before you start eating is an example of:
      a.   mores
      b.   ethnocentrism
      c.   folkways
      d.   laws

18.   Which of the following is an example of mores?
      a.   the incest taboo
      b.   refusing to salute the flag
      c.   driving above the speed limit
      d.   forgetting to attend a cousin's wedding

19.   According to the text's discussion of cultural change in China:
      a.   today, the Communist Party is a "kinder, gentler government"
      b.   the number of Chinese living in absolute poverty has dropped substantially in recent years
      c.   most of China's population has had direct experience with political repression
      d.   there has been little cultural change in China over the past few decades

20.   The militia movement that came to public attention after the bombing of the federal building in Oklahoma City is an example of a:
a.   contraculture
b.   cultural relativity
c.   symbolism
d.   counterculture

Answers

1.   c: No other species is as dependent on learning as humans. The different ways we adapt to the environment, communicate, select mates, and rear young depend on cultural learning, not instinct. (Culture: An Overview; pp. 84-85)

2.   d: Cultures consist of six main elements: beliefs, values, norms and sanctions, symbols, language, and technology. (The Elements of Culture (p. 87)

3.   b: Answers a and d are drawn from Vietnamese culture, but they describe beliefs and practices, not values; answer c is an American value. (The Elements of Culture; pp. 87-89)

4.   d: To westerners, female genital mutilation is a cruel, barbaric, dangerous practice--the ultimate form of female oppression. For those who engage in the practice, including the women themselves, their reaction is simply: "This is our custom, part of our traditions, something we've always done." Such is the nature of cultural relativity. (*Sociology and the Media:* "Female Genital Mutilation: Rites versus Rights"; pp. 98-100)

5.   b: Judging by the number of Americans who delay marriage in order to *play the field*, seek divorces, and engage in extramarital flirtations, if not affairs, this is an ideal we honor in the breach. (Cultural Inconsistencies and Diversities; pp. 97-98)

6.   c: Informal sanctions are still important in modern societies, but the role of formal sanctions has increased. (Norms and Sanctions; p. 91)

7.   b: Symbols are things that can express or evoke meaning; many are physical objects that have acquired cultural meaning and are used for symbolic rather than instrumental purposes. (The Elements of Culture; 91-92)

8.   c: Values are abstract standards or ideals.   The other answers

describe specific guidelines for behavior, or norms. (The Elements of Culture; pp. 88-90)

9.   c: This policy was based on the unquestioned assumption that mainstream American culture is vastly superior to Native American culture. (Ethnocentrism and Cultural Relativism; p. 95)

10.   d: Both norms and values are shared standards; both may be routinely ignored in everyday behavior. The difference between them is that values are abstract standards whereas norms are concrete rules. (The Elements of Culture; p. 90)

11.   a: Beliefs are shared ideas about cause and effect--in this case, the idea that male genes promote strength. The notion that men should, therefore, carry heavy packages for women is a norm derived from this belief. Not all cultures share this view; in some, women are expected to perform most heavy labor. (The Elements of Culture; pp. 87-88)

12.   b: Functionalists emphasize the role of culture in promoting social solidarity and adaptation to the environment. (Explaining Culture; pp. 103-104)

13.   c: Conflict theorists maintain that the dominant culture in a society usually benefits some groups at the expense of others. (Explaining Culture; 104-105)

14.   a: Sapir and Whorf argued that language helps to determine how we see the world. (Language; p. 93)

15.   d: Norms are rules about what people should and should not do, say, or think in a given situation. Values are broad, abstract, shared standards of what is right, desirable, and worthy of respect. (Norms and Sanctions; pp. 90-91)

16.   c: The simultaneous belief in the rule *Thou shalt not kill* and the rule *an eye for an eye* is an example of internal contradictions in culture. (Cultural Inconsistencies and Diversities; pp. 97-98)

17.   c: Folkways are conventions or habits that people follow without giving much thought to what they are doing or why. (Norms and Sanctions; p. 90)

18.   a: Mores are rules for behavior that people consider sacred. Although all of the other answers describe violations of norms and laws, none of these actions is considered *unthinkable* except incest. (The Elements of Culture; p. 90)

19.   b: The future of China is uncertain, but it is clear that culturally,

China will never be the same again. (The Case of China; pp. 111-113)

20. d: In some instances, subcultures do not merely differ from the mainstream, but actively oppose the values and practices of the larger society. "Counterculture" means "against the culture." (Subcultures and Countercultures; p. 101)

CRITICAL THINKING

1. Many elements of our culture are so much a part of our everyday environment that we don't realize how pervasively they affect our present and future lives. Consider two important elements of our material culture -- the car and the television. How have they changed American society? Your own life? On balance, would you say they have been more beneficial than harmful? Try the same exercise with some aspect of our nonmaterial culture such as (1) the notion that the spread of communism must be checked by the United States or (2) the Judeo-Christian belief in a single God.

2. Let's assume that you are interested in the production of culture. In particular, you want to learn more about the production of textbooks. Who decides which textbooks are published? Who decides, for example, which topics and studies are included in a sociology text? What are the consequences of such decisions? How would you go about studying the production of textbooks?

WEB EXERCISE: Exploring the Oklahoma City Bombing Incident

The text cites the bombing of a federal building in Oklahoma City as an example of domestic terrorism and related to the militia movement in American culture. The militia movement is an example of a *counterculture*. The following web site offers a dramatic glimpse of the tragedy in Oklahoma City:

http://www.terrorism.com/terrorism/okc.html

This site is also an excellent source of information on domestic terrorism in general and offers substantial insight into the phenomenon of countercultural activities in the United States.

Chapter Four

SOCIALIZATION THROUGH THE
LIFE COURSE

OBJECTIVES

After reading Chapter Four, you should be able to provide detailed answers to the following questions:

1.   How important is socialization?
2.   How does socialization occur?
3.   How do heredity and the social environment shape human development?
4.   How do Freud's views of socialization differ from those of Cooley and Mead?
5.   What are the major agents of socialization?
6.   How does socialization extend over the life cycle?

CHAPTER REVIEW

I.   What is socialization/how important is it?

Socialization is education in the broadest sense: it is the lifelong process of social interaction that can transform an infant into a child thirsting for knowledge, perhaps a rebellious teenager, a worker, a spouse and parent, and eventually into an elder member of society. The text employs a brief biography of the well-known anthropologist Margaret Mead to illustrate the many changes that people undergo as they mature and grow older. The remainder of the chapter deals with how and why these changes occur, beginning with some very basic questions and answers about human behavior.

The debate concerning *nature and nurture* dates back to the turn of the century. Social Darwinists (and others) argued that a person's character and position in society are genetically determined. Behaviorists countered that experience is *everything*. Contemporary sociologists have developed a synthesis, wherein both extremes of genetic and social environmental determinism are rejected. Instead, they see development as a result of the interaction of genetic potential and socially derived factors. Genes establish potential and limits. How much potential is realized depends upon socialization.

The text describes two main sources of evidence that support the importance of socialization: studies of children raised in near total isolation (the real-life equivalent of myths of feral children purported to have been raised by wild animals), and cross-cultural comparisons (such as Margaret Mead's study of sex and temperament in different societies). If human behavior were genetically determined, children would develop characteristically *human* behavior patterns, *with or without* social interaction; and males and females in one culture would behave in much the same way as their counterparts in another. Rather obviously, this is not the case. The nature-nurture debate will not disappear, however, and articles related to this subject continue to appear in news and popular publications. Some of the strongest evidence for the impact of socialization comes from neurobiology. Heredity sets the stage for human development, but socialization writes the script.

II.   How Does Socialization Occur?

Your text examines two contrasting perspectives on socialization, each of which focuses on different aspects of human development:

A.   The psychologist Sigmund Freud was primarily interested in personality: how the individual develops characteristic ways of thinking and behaving. Freud viewed socialization as a confrontation between a child's innate sexual and aggressive urges and the demands of parents and others to act *civilized*. The child is saying, *I will*; society, typically through the child's parents, is saying *No, you won't*; and the resolution of these types of conflicts determines how the individual will handle future situations. The social control of sexual impulses plays a central role in Freud's theories. He fashioned five critical stages in personality development: the oral, anal, latency, phallic, and genital. In mature individuals, the *ego* mediates between the asocial, pleasure-seeking *id* and the punitive, guilt-ridden *superego*. Freud envisioned the *libido* as the driving force, but recognized that family interactions play a major role in personality development. Few social scientists dispute Freud's brillance or his profound influence on contemporary thought, but many question the scientific validity of his analysis.

B.   Charles Horton Cooley and George Herbert Mead were primarily interested in social development; that is, how social interaction shapes the individual's identity or sense of self. Cooley showed that our self-images are largely a reaction to what we see in other people's responses toward us (the *looking-glass self*). Mead identified two principal stages in the development of the self: the *play stage*, in which children learn to *take the role of the other* (and role model after *significant others*); and the *game stage*, in which children learn to participate in reciprocal relationships through games (and develop a *generalized other*). Mead distinguished between the impulsive, creative *I* and the *me*, which seeks social approval.

Both Mead and Cooley saw socialization as a cooperative effort in which the individual develops a sense of self in relationship to others and society is recreated as a generalized other in the individual's mind.

III.   The Major Agents of Socialization

The text identifies five primary agents of socialization that operate both independently and interdependently: the family, school, peer groups, mass media, and reference groups.

A.   The *family* is perhaps the most basic agent of socialization in that it is the first, and possibly the most important, influence on the individual. Different styles of parenting (authoritarian, permissive, and authoritative) have been linked to social class differences. Parents socialize their children into the world they know, the one into which they (the parents) have been socialized, and with which they are most comfortable.

B.   The *school* gives youngsters experience in dealing with a large, bureaucratic organization in which the same rules are supposed to apply to everyone and individuals are valued in terms of their performance.

C.   The importance of *peers* increases with age. Peers provide young people with their first experience with egalitarian relationships, opportunities to test what they are taught by adults, and group support for developing alternative norms and values.

D.   The *mass media* (especially television) is an extremely controversial agent of socialization. There is evidence that violence on primetime programs encourages aggressive behavior and that commercials promote sex stereotyping.   But there is also evidence that TV can encourage pro-social behavior and provide positive models.

E.   *Reference groups* are used by individuals both as models and as measures of self-worth as they move through the life cycle; these groups may be positive or negative.

IV.   How does socialization change over the life cycle?

The psychologist Erik Erikson was one of the first social scientists to examine systematically the changes people undergo following adolescence. He viewed each stage in life as presenting new crises that require new adjustments. The text uses his description of the *eight stages of man* as a framework for considering socialization over the life cycle.

A.   Erikson saw the central crises of childhood as establishing basic trust (vs. mistrust), autonomy (vs. shame and doubt), initiative (vs. guilt), industry (vs. inferiority). Like the theorists considered earlier in the chapter, Erikson was concerned with *every child*. Sociologists point out, however, that not every child's experiences are alike.

B.   Erikson saw the central task of adolescence as establishing identity (vs. role confusion). Sociological analysis shows that adolescence as we know it is largely a social invention. In other cultures, where individuals do not have to create their own identities and adults are not so ambivalent about teenage sexuality, the transition from childhood to adulthood can be smooth.   The identity crisis many young people experience in our society can be traced, first, to the ambiguous role occupied by adolescents (teenagers are neither children nor adults), and second, to the necessity of choosing from among a wide array of life styles and occupations.

C.   Erikson saw the central task of adulthood as establishing intimacy (vs. isolation), generativity (vs. stagnation), and integrity (vs. despair). This orderly progression was based on the assumption that most people would finish school and settle down into a career and family, their children would leave home at a certain time, and so on. Things have changed in American society since Erikson first developed his theory. The ages at which individuals attain the traditional markers of adulthood have changed. Norms governing sexual activity have changed, as have work habits. Young adults are postponing the assumption of full-scale roles, and the roles of men and women have been altered dramatically.

Daniel Levinson has also examined adult roles and finds that men's and women's behaviors have changed over the years. He sees adulthood as a series of crises, of which the most notable is the *midlife crisis*: the last chance to *make it*. Some researchers maintain that the female equivalent of the male midlife crisis is the *empty nest syndrome*: the dissatisfaction and depression that women may feel at midlife when their children leave home, their husbands are still engrossed in careers, and they go through *menopause*. There is substantial controversy over whether menopause is a medical crisis or simply a change. Sociologist Alice Rossi has concluded that the "crisis," if there is one, is neither biological nor medical. Rather, it results from normal aging and from women's fear of losing their sex appeal, not from menopause itself. But she adds that social expectations can function as a self-fulfilling prophecy. There is even some recent concern with male menopause.

As our society experiences an increase in the number of elderly people, the social meaning of reaching age sixty-five has changed. Later adulthood is no longer a period of despair and isolation for many. There are more older Americans in better health than ever before, and they are more active. The result is a restructuring of retirement so that it may be enjoyed in the company of others in a similar situation for an increasing number of elderly people.

In the not very distant past, death was a taboo subject among Americans. The writings of Elisabeth Kubler-Ross and Ira Byok have broken this silence, and their books have stimulated more research interest in Americans' attitudes toward death.

CONCEPT REVIEW

Match each of the following terms with the correct definition.

a.	self (p. 129)	i.	game stage (p. 130)
b.	play stage (p. 130)	j.	menopause (p. 149)
c.	reference group (p. 131)	k.	the "I" (p. 131)
d.	looking-glass self (p. 129)	l.	resocialization (p. 146)
e.	personality (p. 128)	m.	symbolic interaction (p. 130)
f.	anticipatory socialization (p. 134)	n.	primary groups (p. 130)
		o.	socialization (p. 122)
g.	agent of socialization (p. 131)	p.	generalized other (p. 131)
		q.	taking the role of the other (p. 130)
h.	rites of passage (p. 142)		

r.   the "me" (p. 131)   u.   significant others (p. 131)
s.   identity crisis (p. 143)   v.   ego (p. 129)
t.   superego (p. 129)   w.   id (p. 129)

1.___   The individual's sense of identity or *who I am*.
2.___   The individual's characteristic patterns of behavior and thought.
3.___   George Herbert Mead's term for the stage in social development when children begin to participate in reciprocal relationships with others.
4.___   The socialized self that is composed of internalized norms and values and is ever mindful of its social reflection.
5.___   Charles Horton Cooley's term for the images we have of ourselves, based upon our observations of how other people react toward us.
6.___   The process of putting oneself in the other person's shoes.
7.___   The symbolic communications contained in a smile or a frown, a hug or a slap, and especially, in language.
8.___   The process whereby one acquires a sense of personal identity and learns what people in the surrounding culture believe and how they expect one to behave.
9.___   Groups like the family which are characterized by "intimate face-to-face associations" and "mutual identification."
10.___   Rituals or ceremonies to mark the transition of one stage of life to another.
11.___   The inability to reconcile the image people have of themselves with actual skills, potential, and activities, or with the image they have based on other people's expectations.
12.___   George Herbert Mead's term for the internalized image of the structure and norms of society as a whole.
13.___   George Herbert Mead's term for the impulsive, creative, selfish part of the self.
14.___   The cessation of ovulation and menstruation in human females.
15.___   Learning about and practicing a new role before one is actually in a position to play that role.
16.___   The process of "unlearning" norms and values that were adaptive and considered culturally appropriate in the past in order to take on new social positions and roles.
17.___   A group or social category that individuals use as a guide in developing their values, attitudes, behavior, and self-image.

18.___ A group or social category that an individual uses as a guide in developing his/her values, attitudes, behavior, and self-image.

19.___ George Herbert Mead's term for the stage in social development when children first engage in imitative play and then begin to take the role of the other.

20.___ The reservoir of innate, primitive, asocial, sexual and aggressive urges with which a child is born.

21.___ The rational part of the personality that deals with the outside world, channels impulses from the id into socially acceptable activities, and protects the individual from impossible demands from the superego.

22.___ People whose evaluations an individual holds in high esteem.

23.___ The internal representation of society's norms and values, especially as taught by the child's parents (It is roughly the equivalent to what we call the "conscience").

Answers

1.	a	9.	n	17.	g
2.	e	10.	h	18.	c
3.	i	11.	s	19.	b
4.	r	12.	p	20.	w
5.	d	13.	k	21.	v
6.	q	14.	j	22.	u
7.	m	15.	f	23.	t
8.	o	16.	l		

REVIEW QUESTIONS

1. Most social scientists today would agree with the statement:

   a. Human behavior is largely determined by genes, acting independently of the environment.

   b. Human behavior is largely determined by experience and learning, acting independently of genes.

   c. Genes and environment interact in the process of human development.

   d. Genes and environment have little effect on human development, which is the result of socialization.

2.   Some of the strongest evidence for the impact of socialization comes from the field of:
      a.   exobotany
      b.   zoology
      c.   neurobiology
      d.   physics

3.   By *taking the role of the other*, George Herbert Mead meant:
      a.   practicing a new role before actually taking on that role
      b.   seeing an image of oneself reflected in other people's eyes
      c.   learning to play a game, such as baseball, by the rules
      d.   putting oneself in the other person's shoes

4.   Erik Erikson saw the achievement of identity as a prerequisite for _____ in young adulthood.
      a.   identity
      b.   intimacy
      c.   industry
      d.   integrity

5.   One of the primary differences between peers and parents as agents of socialization is that:
      a.   peers engage in open conflict
      b.   peer relationships are egalitarian
      c.   peers and parents have different, conflicting values
      d.   peers are more fun

6.   Some adolescents are unable to reconcile the image they have of themselves with their actual skills, potential, and activities or with the image of themselves they see reflected in other people's eyes. This behavior reflects:
      a.   unconscious modeling
      b.   identity formation
      c.   the development of significant others
      d.   an identity crisis

7. Socialization involves:
    a. unconscious modeling
    b. explicit instruction
    c. acquiring a sense of identity
    d. all of the above processes

8. Freud's term for the part of the personality that operates on the pleasure principle, seeking immediate gratification, is the:
    a. id
    b. ego
    c. superego
    d. libido

9. Your mother has asked you to visit an uncle who is in the hospital. You discover that a movie you have been wanting to see is on TV that night. You're torn, but you decide to visit your uncle. According to George Herbert Mead, which part of the self governed your behavior?
    a. the significant other
    b. the "me"
    c. the generalized other
    d. the "I"

10. Which of the following theorists saw socialization as a confrontation between the individual and society?
    a. Sigmund Freud
    b. Erik Erikson
    c. George Herbert Mead
    d. Charles Horton Cooley

11. In his study of class differences in socialization, Kohn found that:
    a. middle-class parents are more concerned about their child's performance in school than working-class parents are
    b. middle-class parents are less concerned about neatness and obedience than working-class parents are
    c. middle-class parents are more concerned about teaching their children how to get ahead than working-class parents are
    d. working-class parents do a better job of socialization than middle-class parents do

12.   According to Cooley, the *looking-glass self* consists of:
a.   how we imagine others see us
b.   how we imagine others judge us
c.   how we feel about the reactions of others
d.   all of the above

13.   Young children "play" at being mothers and fathers, cops and robbers, Hollywood stars and sports heroes. All of these examples of role playing illustrate:
a.   the generalized other
b.   learning to play the game
c.   anticipatory socialization
d.   id impulses

14.   Jim's father is a senior partner in a large Washington law firm; his mother is head of a Virginia school district. Most of their friends are as successful and career-oriented as they are. Jim has no interest in what he sees as the *rat race*; he wants to be a cabinetmaker. His parents' circle of friends serve as a:
a.   primary group
b.   looking-glass self
c.   positive reference group
d.   negative reference group

15.   According to George Herbert Mead, the primary change in the game stage of social development is that:
a.   children learn to take the role of the other
b.   children acquire a generalized other
c.   children learn to play by the rules
d.   the *me* and the *I* become differentiated

16.   Which of the following is NOT one of Diana Baumrind's distinct styles of parenting?
a.   authoritarian
b.   permissive
c.   egalitarian
d.   authoritative

17.   Which of the following is NOT one of the stages of death, according to Elisabeth Kubler-Ross?
    a.   rejection
    b.   bargaining
    c.   depression
    d.   denial

18.   Young people are exposed to violence not only in movies and sit- coms but also in the increasingly popular "_____," which feature reality-based footage of violence.
    a.   slasher films
    b.   shockumentaries
    c.   zappers
    d.   talking-heads

19.   Daniel Levinson and Judith Levinson collected life stories from 45 women approaching middle age. In comparing these women's patterns of adult development with men's, these researchers discovered that
    a.   men's and women's experiences are dramatically different
    b.   women have a more severe mid-life transition than men
    c.   women go through the same sequence of eras as men and at the same ages.
    d.   none of the above

20.   Most studies find that depression is a/an _____ of menopausal problems in women.
    a.   predictor
    b.   consequence
    c.   end product
    d.   cause

Answers

1.   c: Most social scientists reject both genetic determinism and environmental determinism as oversimiplifications of a complex process. (The Nature of Human Behavior; pp. 123-124)

2.   c: Recent advances in research technology have enabled scientists to study the development of the brain in some detail: From the moment of birth, experience washes through the brain in waves and experience is the key. (The Impact of Socialization; p. 128)

3.   d: Mead saw the first evidence of this in the play stage, when children pretend to be other people. He maintained that children begin to develop a sense of self only when they discover how it feels to be another person. Only then do they see themselves as social objects. (The Emergence of Self; p. 130)

4.   b: Erikson saw the achievement of identity as a prerequisite for intimacy in young adulthood. Until young people are sure of who they are, they do not feel secure enough to make a commitment to another person.(Socialization and the Life Cycle; pp. 141-142)

5.   b: Parents and children often run into conflicts (a); Children often devise and enforce strict rules for their games (c); Peers can be as demanding, hurtful, or dull as parents (d).   (Agents of Socialization; pp. 132-135)

6.   d: Lacking a firm identity, adolescents may over-identify with others, hoping to find an identity in their connection to others, such as celebrities. (Socialization and the Life Cycle; p. 143)

7.   d: The term *socialization* covers the whole range of social activities and experiences that contribute to transforming an infant into a participating member of society. (The Nature of Human Behavior; p. 122)

8.   a: Freud saw the id as a reservoir of primitive, infantile urges, caged in the process of socialization, but never entirely tamed. (The Process of Socialization: Psychosexual Development; p. 129)

9.   b: According to Mead, the *me* is the social self, the part of a person that seeks social approval. If the *I*--the spontaneous, self-centered part of the self--had been in control, you would have watched the movie. (The Emergence of Self; pp. 130-131)

10.   a: Freud viewed socialization as a taming of the human animal, but

he also believed that civilization was a continuing source of discontent. (Psychosexual Development: Freud; pp. 128-129)

11.   b: Most parents want their children to do well in school and to get ahead in life, but their own experiences have taught them different routes to success (initiative in the middle-class world; obedience in the working-class world). (Agents of Socialization; p. 133)

12.   d: Cooley believed that our self-image depends not only on the image of ourselves that we see reflected in others' eyes, but also on our reactions to those judgments. If someone you do not consider very intelligent tells you that you are "stupid," for example, it won't damage your self-esteem. If a significant other makes the same comment, it will have an effect. (The Emergence of Self; pp. 129-130)

13.   c: Much of children's play (alone and together) may be described as anticipatory socialization: learning about and practicing a new role before they are in a position to play the role. (Agents of Socialization; p. 134)

14.   d: Reference groups can be positive or negative. Jim's self-image is based in part on those people he does not want to resemble. (Agents of Socialization; pp. 131-132)

15.   b: Mead used the image of a game to describe this stage, because to play an organized game like baseball, a child must understand the relationship between the position he/she is playing and the other positions. In other words, the child must have a general image of the game. (The Emergence of Self; pp. 129-131)

16.   c: Baumrind identified three distinct styles of parenting: authoritarian, permissive, and authoritative. (Agents of Socialization-The Family; pp. 132-133)

17.   a: Kubler-Ross's stages of dying are: denial, anger, bargaining, depression, and acceptance. (Facing Death; p. 153)

18.   b: The extremely popular "Cops" is a good example of a "shockumentary," because it contains reality-based footage of various forms of violent behavior. (Agents of Socialization; p. 136)

19.   c: Daniel Levinson and Judith Levinson's second study surprised these researchers when they found that women go through the same sequence of patterns in adult development. (Socialization

and the Life Cycle; pp. 146-149)

20.   a: Most studies find that depression is more likely to be a predictor of menopausal problems than a consequence (Socialization and the Life Cycle; pp. 149-150)

CRITICAL THINKING

1.   Most discussions of socialization emphasize the role that parents play in socializing their children. But it could also be argued that *children socialize their parents*. Think about how the arrival of a child changes a husband's and wife's self-images, social identities, life styles, and relationships with each other. Think about how the departure of the children for college or marriage changes their relationship. What does this tell you about socialization?

2.   Traditionally, the family has been the major agent of socialization in the United States. Has the family's influence on socialization been increasing or decreasing in recent decades? What roles traditionally filled by the family have been assumed by other agents? How do you think such changes will affect social relations in our society?

WEB EXERCISE: Homosexuality: Nature or Nurture?

The *Close-Up* insert in this chapter is entitled "Homosexuality: Born or Bred?" After you have read this installment, access the following site on the Internet:

http://www.afa.net/homosexuality

This site provides a variety of opportunities to evaluate the "myths and facts" about homosexuality, including the extent of what is known about the "causes" of sexual orientation. As you explore the site, pay special attention to materials that focus on the "nature or nurture" question.

Chapter Five

SOCIAL STRUCTURE

OBJECTIVES

After reading Chapter Five, you should be able to provide detailed answers to the following questions:

1. What is social structure?
2. How does social structure affect individual behavior?
3. What are the basic building blocks of social structure?
4. How do social structures provide the framework of societies?
5. How have societies and relations among societies changed over time?

CHAPTER REVIEW

I. What is social structure?

Social structure refers to the relatively stable and enduring patterns that organize social relationships and provide the basic framework for what we call "society." The text uses the recently established Women's National Basketball Association to illustrate this concept. In the first place, the WNBA has altered the structure of professional basketball in American society. Similar to other professional athletic organizations, players are assigned to specialized, interdependent positions and these players are expected to observe the rules of the game. These structural principles transform a collection of people on offense, defense, and special teams into a working unit that has specific goals. In much the same fashion, social structure transforms an assortment of people into groups, a population into society.

There are two basic approaches to studying social structure: the *microperspective*, providing a close-up, detailed analysis of what people do, say, and think; and the *macroperspective*, which is used to analyze the overall patterns and long-term trends of societies.

II.   How does social structure affect individual behavior?

The central question, at the heart of sociology, is: *How does social structure affect individual and group behavior?* The text utilizes basketball once again to provide concrete illustrations of social structure at work. The structure of positions and roles enables players to function as a team, coordinating their activities. This discussion also compares men's and women's basketball, illustrating how social structure casts individuals into different roles, but does not determine how they play their parts or prevent them from changing the rules and breaking through boundaries.

III.   What are the basic building blocks of social structure?

Relationships are the basic building blocks of social structure. Sociologists use the term *status* to describe a position an individual occupies in society. In everyday conversation, people typically use the word status to refer to prestige. For sociologists, status refers to any position in society, high or low. Some social statuses are *achieved*, or attained through personal effort; others are *ascribed*, or assigned to the individual at birth or at different stages in the life cycle. A *master status* is that which overrides other characteristics of a person. It is the position with which an individual is most identified.

A *role* is the collection of culturally defined rights, obligations, and expectations that accompany a status in the social system. If you occupy the status of "student," for example, you are expected to play the part of a student. As on the stage, a role establishes guidelines; how different individuals interpret a role will vary. A single status establishes a number of different relationships which are known collectively as a *role set*. Thus, a professor is expected to play the role of teacher with students, colleagues, other faculty members, employees, the university administration, and so on. Moreover, an individual occupies a number of different statuses at the same time (professor, spouse, neighbor, African American). Roles simplify social interaction, but may also lead to *strain*, when an individual is unable to fill a role; or *conflict*, when different roles make incompatible demands.

Statuses and roles lay the foundations for *social relationships*: connections between individuals that are shaped by intersecting roles and patterned interaction. Relationships take many forms. *Groups* are made up of a number of individuals who feel a common identity and interact in a regular and structured way, on the basis of shared norms and goals. Groups come in many shapes and sizes and are described in detail in Chapter 6 of this text. When a group grows beyond a certain size, or when a goal requires the coordinated skills and efforts of a number of people, a *formal organization* is likely to emerge: a group designed to pursue specific goals, and held together by explicit rules and regulations. The text uses professional basketball as an example of the importance and impact of formal organizations. All large-scale organizations share certain characteristics: formal structure, participants, goals, and technology

Bureaucracies are hierarchical organizations that are governed by formal rules and regulations. Today, the word "bureaucrat" strikes many as unpleasant and insulting.

Sociologist Max Weber was one of the first to recognize the importance of bureaucracy to the large organizations of modern society. His model of bureaucracy was conceived as an ideal type: it was meant to capture the essential characteristics of bureaucratic organization rather than how one *ought* to be configured. For Weber, bureaucracy has six key features: a clear-cut division of labor, a clearly defined hierarchy and authority, formal rules and regulations, impersonality, positions based on technical qualifications and performance, and a clear line between the public and private spheres.

Virtually all bureaucratic organizations have both a *formal* and an *informal* structure. The *formal structure* consists of official rules and regulations, explicit job descriptions, and the like, while the *informal structure* consists of unofficial norms and personal relationships. Bureaucracies have a number of dysfunctions, including their dependence on routinization, the tendency to promote trained incapacity, depersonalization, and vested interests. Weber's friend and colleague, Robert Michels, coined the *iron law of oligarchy*, implying that very large organizations tend to concentrate power in the hands of a few.

IV.   The Structure of Society

A *society* is an autonomous group of people who occupy a common territory and have a common culture and a sense of shared identity. Societies are held together by relationships, not only among people but also among institutions. *Social institutions* are stable sets of norms and values, statuses and roles, and groups and organizations that provide a structure for behavior in a particular area of social life. The five major social institutions in modern societies--the family, education, religion, politics, economics--all perform basic social functions. Each institution deals with a different aspect of life; they are all interrelated; and each is part of an integrated whole. Because social institutions are interconnected, change in one invariably leads to change in others. Institutions establish links between the past, present, and future; they give social life continuity.

      An equally pervasive feature of human societies is structured inequality. *Social stratification* refers to the division of society into layers or social classes who have unequal access to wealth, power, and prestige. Americans, in particular, pride themselves on being a free society in which people earn their position in life, whether high or low.   Socioeconomic, racial and ethnic, and gender discrimination are examined in detail in Chapters 8, 9, and 10. In this discussion, age stratification is discussed: All societies use age as a basis for assigned rights and privileges; an individual's position in the life cycle in part determines the roles that are available. Age grades are ascribed statuses over which the individual has no control, as is the case with sex, race, and ethnicity. All of the foregoing are also master statuses that tend to override most other traits. The lowered status of elderly people is reflected in *ageism*: subtle (and not very subtle) forms of prejudice and discrimination against older people. There is a great deal of age discrimination in employment. While many older Americans in the U.S. today enjoy a higher standard of living than did any previous generation of elderly Americans, there is still a great deal of age inequality.

V.   Relations Among Societies

      No society exists in isolation. Some sociologists, like Gerhard Lenski and Jean Lenski, view the history of society as a process of sociocultural evolution, from simpler to more complex forms. Four basic types of societies have emerged over the course of human history: *hunter-gatherer bands, horticultural villages, agrarian states* and, most recently, *industrial societies*.

A. For 99 percent of human history, our ancestors lived as hunters and gatherers. They neither produced nor preserved their food, and lived in nomadic bands of ten to fifty people. There were no formal political or economic institutions in these types of societies. Individuals earned respect for their skills; every adult male was a hunter, and the adult females were gatherers. There was a high degree of freedom; no one worked for anyone else. Warfare was unknown because the human population was small and natural resources abundant. When bands did not get along with each other, they simply moved apart.

B. About 10,000 years ago, human beings became food producers for the first time. The domestication of plants and animals is associated with the first settled villages, more complex social structure, and war. There were no formal political, economic, or religious institutions in these villages, but the beginnings were there.

C. The agricultural revolution, which began about 6,000 years ago, paved the way for a new and more intricate type of society: the agrarian state. The plow and other inventions made it possible to keep land in continuous cultivation, to establish permanent settlements, and to produce a food surplus. This, in turn, made it possible for some members of the population to devote themselves full-time to activities other than farming.

The rise of agrarian states is associated with the first cities. Agrarian states were far more complex than any society known before. The size of society increased; territory expanded; new institutions arose (religion, politics, and economics); and the number of statuses and roles multiplied. The vast majority of the peoples in these societies were peasants.

D. The industrial nation is a comparatively recent invention. The Industrial Revolution, which began in England about 200 years ago, reshaped social structure in a number of ways. Tasks once performed by humans were soon performed by machines, on assembly lines, at a much faster speed and lower cost. Changes in the structure of work had a profound impact on the structure of society, especially the changes in social institutions.

Some sociologists maintain that in the second half of the twentieth century, a new type of "postindustrial" society has emerged.

A *world system* is an economic network that links the nations of the world into a single socioeconomic unit; there are three positions in this system: *core nations, peripheral nations, and semiperipheral nations.* A nation's position in the world system determines not only its economic well-being, but also many features of its internal social structure.

CONCEPT REVIEW

Match each of the following terms with the correct definition.

a.   role strain (p. 168)
b.   microperspective (p. 160)
c.   ageism (p. 184)
d.   status (p. 166)
e.   society (p. 185)
f.   groups (p. 170)
g.   role (p. 167)
h.   social institution (p. 179)
i.   achieved status (p. 166)
j.   ascribed status (P. 166)
k.   iron law of oligarchy (p. 178)

l.   formal organization (p. 170)
m.   social stratification (p. 175)
n.   ideal type (p. 175)
o.   world system (p. 191)
p.   role set (p. 168)
q.   bureaucracy (p. 174)
r.   role conflict (p. 168)
s.   macroperspective (p. 160)
t.   master status (p. 160)
u.   social structure (p. 160)

1.___   A "wide-angle lens" to analyze the overall patterns and long-term trends of populations, societies, and the world as a whole.
2.___   What occurs when the different positions an individual occupies make incompatible demands.
3.___   An autonomous population whose members are subject to the same political authority, occupy a common territory, and have a common culture and a sense of shared identity.
4.___   A position in the social structure as opposed to functioning within the structure.
5.___   The cluster of different social relationships in which a person becomes involved because he or she occupies a particular social status.
6.___   A social status that is attained through personal effort.
7.___   Occurs when a single status makes contradictory or conflicting demands makes contradictory or conflicting demands on a person.
8.___   The relatively stable and enduring patterns that organize social relationships and provide the basic framework for what we call "society."
9.___   A "zoom lens" that yields close-up, detailed analysis of what people do, say, and think in the actual flow of momentary experience.
10.___   A hierarchical organization that is governed by formal rules and

regulations.

11.___ A social status that is assigned to an individual at birth or at different stages of the life cycle.

12.___ A social status that tends to override everything else the person is or does in life.

13.___ Describes subtle (and not very subtle) forms of prejudice and discrimination against older people.

14.___ A number of people who feel a common identity and interact in a regular and structured way, on the basis of shared norms and goals.

15.___ Stable and enduring sets of norms, values, statuses, roles, groups, and organizations that provide a structure for behavior in a particular area of social life.

16.___ The collection of culturally defined rights, obligations, and expectations that accompany a status in a social system.

17.___ An economic network that links the nations of the world into a single socioeconomic unit.

18.___ A group designed and created to pursue specific goals, and held together by explicit rules and regulations.

19.___ The division of a society into layers or social classes who have unequal access to wealth, power, and prestige.

20.___ A principle fashioned by Robert Michels, arguing that even the most democratic, idealistic organizations will inevitably become "ruled by a few."

21.___ A number of people who feel a common identity and interact in a regular and structured way, on the basis of shared norms and goals.

Answers

1.	s	9.	b	17.	o
2.	i	10.	q	18.	l
3.	e	11.	j	19.	m
4.	d	12.	t	20.	k
5.	p	13.	c	21.	n
6.	i	14.	f		
7.	a	15.	h		
8.	v	16.	g		

REVIEW QUESTIONS

1.   Which of the following statements about social structure is FALSE?
        a.   Social structure provides continuity.
        b.   Social structure determines the outcome of social interaction.
        c.   Social structure shapes everyday behavior.
        d.   Social structure transforms a collection of people into a group, community, or society.

2.   Four basic types of societies have emerged over the course of human history. Which of the following is NOT one of these?
        a.   hunter-gatherer bands
        b.   horticultural villages
        c.   industrial nations
        d.   preindustrial societies

3.   Which of the following is an example of an achieved status?
        a.   wife
        b.   brother
        c.   having blue eyes
        d.   being born male

4.   The basic elements of social structure are:
        a.   statuses, relationships, roles, and organizations.
        b.   statuses, roles, groups, and organizations.
        c.   roles, groups, organizations, and societies.
        d.   statuses and roles, social relationships, groups, and formal organizations.

5.   A physician's relationships with other physicians, nurses, patients, and patients' families are part of his/her:
        a.   status system
        b.   role
        c.   role set
        d.   identity documents

6.   According to the text's discussion, formal organizations:
       a.   are similar to small groups.
       b.   are held together by folkways.
       c.   tend to be fairly small.
       d.   tend to assume a life of their own, once firmly established.

7.   What is the basic unit of social structure in hunter-gatherer societies?
       a.   family
       b.   band
       c.   clan
       d.   territory

8.   The text points out that all large-scale organizations share certain characteristics, including:
       a.   formal structure
       b.   participants
       c.   goals
       d.   all of the above

9.   Which of the following is NOT one of the dysfunctions of bureaucracy discussed in the text?
       a.   a dependency on routinization
       b.   trained incapacity
       c.   overefficiency
       d.   a built-in tendency toward excessive growth

10.   According to the text's discussion of age discrimination:
       a.   a clear minority of Americans retire, with most continuing to work beyond age 65
       b.   older Americans in the U.S. today have a lower standard of living in comparison with previous generations of elderly Americans
       c.   when they stop working, most older Americans are able to maintain the standard of living that they possessed before retirement.
       d.   none of the above

11.   The political system in the United States is an example of:
   a.   a set of norms and values
   b.   a formal organization
   c.   a social institution
   d.   a set of statuses and roles

12.   Sociologist Immanuel Wallerstein argued that economic relationships extend beyond the borders of nation-states and operate independently of the political systems of those nation-states. The result is:
   a.   a world system
   b.   globalization
   c.   multinational corporations
   d.   interlocking directorates

13.   A sick person's obligation to stay in bed and follow doctor's orders is an example of his or her:
   a.   status
   b.   role
   c.   presentation of self
   d.   institution

14.   Which of the following is NOT one of Wallerstein's positions in the world system?
   a.   core nations
   b.   peripheral nations
   c.   semiperipheral nations
   d.   bilateral nations

15.   The status of U.S. Senator requires that a person represent the people of his or her state and defend their interests; it also requires that the senator consider the best interests of the nation, which may or may not be the same. This predicament illustrates:
   a.   role conflict
   b.   role strain
   c.   identity confusion
   d.   political incorrectness

16.   Social inequality is most pronounced in:
      a.   hunter-gatherer bands
      b.   horticultural societies
      c.   agrarian states
      d.   industrial nations

17.   A mother with a career illustrates role _____: in meeting the
      requirements of a career, she automatically violates the expectation that
      a mother will put her children's needs before everything else; in meeting
      the cultural demands of motherhood, she automatically violates the
      expectation that she will give full attention to her career.
      a.   strain
      b.   incompatibility
      c.   chaos
      d.   conflict

18.   *Senior citizen* is an example of a:
      a.   status
      b.   role
      c.   group
      d.   social institution

19.   In this chapter's *Closeup*, "Are We Prisoners of Society," a social
      psychologist's experiment designed to test popular assumptions about
      prison life is discussed. This classic "prisoner-guard" experiment was
      conducted by:
      a.   Talcott Parsons
      b.   Philip Zimbardo
      c.   Immanuel Wallerstein
      d.   Robert Michels

20.   In this chapter's *A Global View*, "The Japanese Corporation," the text highlights which of the following differences between American and Japanese corporations?
   a.   Japanese corporations' emphasis on lifetime employment
   b.   Japanese corporations' emphasis on collective performance, not individual achievement
   c.   Japanese corporations' holistic concern for employees
   d.   all of the above

Answers

1.   b: Social structure establishes *the rules of the game* and assigns *players* to positions (or statuses), but how individuals play the game depends on their skills, efforts, and imagination. (Introduction; p. 160)

2.   d: The United States was a preindustrial society prior to the late 19th century and was agrarian in focus, but as such, preindustrial societies are not one of the four basic types of societies. (Relations Among Societies; p. 186)

3.   a: An achieved status is a social position that results from the individual's own behavior. It may or may not be considered an *achievement* (a praiseworthy accomplishment) in the eyes of society. (Statuses and Roles; p. 166)

4.   d: Statuses and roles, social relationships, groups, and formal organizations are the basic elements of social structure. (The Basic Elements of Social Structure; p. 164)

5.   c: The status *physician* generates an array of different relationships to people in other statuses (sometimes resulting in role strain or conflict). (Statuses and Roles; pp. 168-169)

6.   d: Formal organizations differ from small groups in their scale, structure, and goal orientation; they are held together by explicit rules and regulations; and they tend to be larger, more complex, and more enduring than informal social groups (Formal Organizations; p. 170).

7.   a: Although the hunter-gatherers lived in bands, membership in a band is flexible. Members were free to come and go as they liked. Thus, the nuclear family was the basic building block of hunter-gatherer societies. (Relations Among Societies; pp. 186-

187)

8.   d: The text discusses four common characteristics of all large-scale organizations: formal structure, participants, goals, and technology. (The Structure of Organizations; p. 173)

9.   c: Bureaucracies are designed to be efficient; dysfunctions include: a dependency on routinization, trained incapacity, depersonalization, vested interests, and a built-in tendency toward excessive growth. (The Structure of Organizations; pp. 178-179)

10.   d: A majority of Americans retire, increasingly before age 65; older Americans in the U.S. today enjoy a higher standard of living than did any previous generation of elderly Americans; and when they stop working, most older Americans see their incomes drop by one-third to one-half. (Social Stratification; p. 184)

11.   c: As an institution, the political system includes norms and values, statuses and roles, groups and formal organizations. The term that describes the entire set of social arrangements is *institution*. (Social Institutions; p. 179)

12.   a: Immanuel Wallerstein pioneered the *world system* approach to the study of social structure and social stratification; a world system is an economic network that links the nations of the world into a single socioeconomic unit. (The World System; p. 191)

13.   b: As Parsons pointed out, someone who does not play the role described here will be evicted from the status of *patient* and considered a malingerer. (Statuses and Roles; p. 167)

14.   d: Wallerstein identified three positions in the world system: *core, peripheral*, and *semiperipheral*. (The World System; pp. 191-192)

15.   b: Role strain occurs when a single status makes contradictory or conflicting demands on a person; role conflict occurs when different roles make competing demands. (The Basic Elements of Social Structure; p. 168)

16.   c: There is very little difference in standard of living from one family to the next in hunter-gatherer bands, and in horticultural villages. And while inequality persists in industrial nations, it is not as extreme in agrarian states, where kings were often treated as gods and peasants and slaves as beasts of burden. (Relations Among Societies; pp. 188-189)

17.   d: Role conflict occurs when different roles make competing demands; role strain occurs when a single status makes contradic-

tory or conflicting demands on a person. (The Basic Elements of Social Structure; p. 168)

18.   a: *Senior citizen* is a position in society, or social status. The role a senior citizen plays depends on the expectations of the people around him/her (whether they feel an older person would be active or take it easy, advise younger relations or acknowledge that they are strangers in the modern world, and so on). (Statuses and Roles; p. 166)

19.   b: Social psychologist Philip Zimbardo's "prisoner-guard" experiment provides a dramatic illustration of how the roles people play shape their thoughts, feelings, and behavior: In everyday life, the roles we play may overpower our principles, our goals, our desires, and even our "personalities." (*Closeup*: "Are We Prisoners of Society?; pp. 164-165)

20.   d: The key differences between American and Japanese corporations involve Japanese corporations' emphasis on: lifetime employment, collective performance, and the holistic concern for employees. (*A Global View:* "The Japanese Corporation; pp. 180-181)

CRITICAL THINKING

1.   At most colleges and universities, students may join a number of different groups, some formally organized (e.g., clubs and societies) and others informally organized (groups of friends who share common interests). Suppose you wanted to join one group of each type. How would your approaches to the two groups differ? In what respects would they be the same? Which would probably be more difficult to join? Why?

2.   Many interpretations of interpersonal interactions in bureaucracies emphasize the dehumanizing influence of the bureaucratic structure. Try considering the issue from a different perspective. How might bureaucracies promote healthy, fulfilling interactions? Overall, would you say that bureaucracies have a more negative than positive influence?

WEB EXERCISE: Learning More About Age Discrimination

In this chapter, *age discrimination* is utilized as an example of social inequality. In your lifetime, you may be affected by this type of discrimination. This exercise encourages you to find out more about this phenomenon via a number of interesting web sites:

The following site, managed by the Department of Health and Human Services, will acquaint you with the Age Discrimination Act and relevant facts concerning age discrimination in the United States:

http://www.os.dhhs.gov/progorg/ocr/age.html

The following three sites are managed by different attorneys at law. These will provide you with a slightly different view of age discrimination: practicing attorneys who are interested in defending clients who believe they have been victimized by this form of discrimination:

http://www15.pair.com/scribe/talklaw/adea.shtml

http://horwitzlaw.com/employ.htm

http://www.collierlaw.com/lol/ageact.shtml

Chapter Six

SOCIAL INTERACTION AND SOCIAL GROUPS

OBJECTIVES

After reading Chapter Six, you should be able to provide detailed responses to the following questions:

1.   How do people establish and maintain rules for social interactions?
2.   How do individuals establish and maintain a social identity?
3.   How do networks take shape?
4.   What is a social group?
5.   What are the main types of social groups?
6.   How does the size of a group affect the way the group functions?
7.   What effect does the structure of a group have on individual and group behavior?

CHAPTER REVIEW

I.   What are the basic elements of social interaction?

In social interaction, one person's actions depend on the actions of another, and vice versa; social interaction is the result of mutual influence. Social interaction is the basis of social organization and structure. Interactions range from the informal to the formal, but all interactions fall into patterns.

The most important and revealing studies of everyday social behavior come from symbolic interactionists, who emphasize the role of language and other symbols in the social construction of identity. Some sociologists in this school draw an analogy between real life and the stage: *the dramaturgical approach* . In many cases, we are so accustomed to our culture's "scripts" (the parts that we play) that we take expected role behavior for granted. Sociologist Harold Garfinkle coined the term *ethnomethodology* in referring to the countless unspoken, often unconscious rules people use to maintain order and predictability in everyday social interaction.

How people interact depends on the situation. When expectations are unclear, people go through a kind of reconciliation process called the *definition of the situation*--an overall idea of what is expected--and this definition establishes a framework for social interaction.

The sociologist Erving Goffman pointed out that there are two main areas of behavior: the public, or *frontstage* and the private, or *backstage*. The text points out, for example, that every marriage has frontstage and backstage ingredients.

Goffman also detailed the *presentation of self*, referring to the ways in which people attempt to direct and control the impressions they make on others and how others see them.

II.   How do individuals establish and maintain a social identity?

A *social identity* is our sense of who and what we are. Social identities are not simply daydreams; they are a major source of plans for action, provide us with the criteria for evaluating our actual performances, and provide meaning to our lives. To affirm a social identity, people strive to "look the part." Clothing fashions distinguish between different groups of people. Fashion and fitness are reflections of cultural ambivalences and unresolved conflicts. Body image ("dress for success") is an important vehicle for social identity in American society. Fitness has become a status symbol, a way of announcing one's social class, as in the expression, "You can never be too rich or too thin."

In all social encounters, participants' identities are on the line. In order to define the situation, participants must *negotiate* who will play which roles and to what degree they will support one another's acts. Goffman used the term *facework* to describe how people tend to support one another's efforts at *managing impressions*.

A number of sociologists see social exchange as the key ingredient in interpersonal relations. The "glue" that binds individuals to one another is the *norm of reciprocity*, which demands that we respond in kind to certain behaviors. Social exchange differs from purely economic exchange in that the terms are subtle and diffuse rather than specific and concrete.

III. How do networks take shape?

A *network* is the web of relationships that connects an individual to many other people, both directly and indirectly. Networks are a familiar part of our everyday lives. There are two approaches to studying networks: a microapproach and a macroapproach. Networks are created through social interaction, but do not depend on frequent contact.

IV. What is the nature of social groups?

"Group" is a multipurpose word. Sometimes, people use it to refer to an *aggregate*, or a collection of people who just happen to be in the same place at the same time. At other times, "group" describes a *social category*: individuals classified together because they share a certain characteristic. A *social group* differs from these haphazard collections of individuals in four ways: Members of a social group have shared identity; they interact regularly; they have a social structure; and they depend on consensus. In other words, a social group is a number of people who feel a common identity and interact in a regular and structured way, on the basis of shared norms and goals. Social groups differ from formal organizations in that they are less formally structured and their rules and goals are less explicit.

V. What are the main types of social groups?

Different kinds of groups carry different meanings. Social groups can be *primary*, and based on intimate personal relationships (e.g., the family), or *secondary*, and based on impersonal, instrumental relationships (e.g., a committee). Within a primary group, there is frequent face-to-face association, with members sharing numerous activities and interests; relationships are valued in themselves. Primary groups are usually small groups with irreplaceable members. Secondary groups, on the other hand, involve occasional face-to-face interaction; relationships are limited and instrumental; and group size is flexible, with replaceable members.

Reference groups are used as a touchstone for evaluating ourselves and monitoring our behavior; they may be primary or secondary, and one does not necessarily have to be a member of a reference group in order to be influenced by it. Reference groups play two main functions: normative and comparative.

In- and out-groups express the idea of "we/us" and "they/them." An in-group is one to which people feel they belong; it commands their loyalty and respect. An out-group is one to which people feel opposed or in competition with.

Peer groups are informal, primary social groups of individuals who share similar characteristics.

VI.   What is the importance of group size?

Numbers have an independent effect on groups; regardless of a group's other characteristics, the addition or subtraction of members will alter relationships. The smallest possible group is the *dyad*, or two-person group; dyads depend on a high degree of commitment and are extremely fragile. *Triads*, or three-person groups, differ from dyads in that triads can suffer the loss of one member and still be a group; and the addition of a third person creates the possibility of coalitions and exclusions.

Without knowing the particular individuals who compose a group, it is possible to predict regular patterns in the emergence of leaders; this is because the way groups are structured has a significant impact on the ways people think and behave. *Instrumental leaders* coordinate activities to meet group goals, while *expressive leaders* specialize in interpersonal relationships.

Groups influence people and a number of processes can be observed, including *social facilitation, social loafing,* and the *reduction of inhibitions*.

Groups tend to produce conformity by putting pressure on dissenters. Some group decision making takes place through a process of *groupthink*, which tends to taint the decision-making process; another pattern of group decision making is the *risky shift*, wherein group members tend to make more daring decisions than they would as individuals. Many studies have shown that group discussion often strengthens participants' original opinions, a phenomenon known as *group polarization*.

CONCEPT REVIEW

Match each of the following terms with the correct definition.

a. aggregate (p. 210)
b. social category (p. 210)
c. social group (p. 210)
d. primary group (p. 211)
e. ethnomethodology (p. 200)
f. reference group (p. 212)
g. secondary group (211)
h. network (p. 207)
i. norm of reciprocity (p. 206)

j. social identity (p. 203)
k. social interaction (p. 199)
l. in-group (p. 213)
m. peer group (p. 214)
n. out-group (p. 213)
o. presentation of self (p. 203)
p. definition of the situation (p. 201)

1. ___ A group that may be primary or secondary and does not require membership that is used as a touchstone for evaluating ourselves and monitoring our behavior.

2. ___ A group one feels opposed to or in competition with.

3. ___ A phenomenon in which one person's actions depend on the actions of the other and vice versa; it is the result of mutual influence, not simply parallel or simultaneous activity.

4. ___ Individuals classified together because they share a certain characteristic.

5. ___ A group to which people feel that they belong; it commands their loyalty and respect.

6. ___ A social group with similar characteristics, whose members are not only the same age and status, but interact frequently.

7. ___ The countless unspoken, often unconscious rules people use to maintain order and predictability in everyday social interaction.

8. ___ A small, warm association based on ongoing, personal, intimate relationships.

9. ___ The web of relationships that connects an individual to many other people, both directly and indirectly.

10. ___ A collection of people who just happen to be in the same place at the same time.

11. ___ Our sense of who and what we are.

12. ___ A group in which the members have shared identity, interact regularly, have a social structure, and depend on consensus.

13. ___ The ways in which people attempt to direct and control the impression

they make on others and on how others see them.

14.___ A "cool" impersonal association whose members' relationships are limited and instrumental; these groups are created to achieve a specific goal.

15.___ The glue that binds individuals to one another, which demands that we respond in kind to certain behavior.

16.___ An overall idea of what is expected, establishing a framework for social interaction.

Answers

1.	f.	7.	e	13.	o
2.	n	8.	d	14.	g
3.	k.	9.	h	15.	i
4.	b	10.	a	16.	p
5.	l.	11.	j		
6.	m	12.	c		

REVIEW QUESTIONS

1. Sociologist Harold Garfinkle invented a technique called "breeching experiment" in which he and his students deliberately violated unspoken assumptions and recorded how other people responded. Through this work, Garfinkle coined the term:
   a.   social interaction
   b.   the definition of the situation
   c.   ethnomethodology
   d.   the norm of reciprocity

2. When groups develop an idea of what is expected, they have arrived at a/an _____, which establishes a framework for social interaction.
   a.   definition of the situation
   b.   ethnomethodology
   c.   norm of reciprocity
   d.   prescribed sanction

3.   A married man and woman who have been arguing constantly for the past two weeks attend a party; while there, they tell their friends that they never fight. This is an example of::
   a.   frontstage behavior
   b.   offstage behavior
   c.   backstage behavior
   d.   the definition of the situation

4.   Sociologist Erving Goffman detailed the *presentation of the self*: the ways in which people attempt to direct and control the impression they make on others and how others see them. Goffman called this:
   a.   frontstage behavior
   b.   backstage behavior
   c.   impression management
   d.   the definition of the situation

5.   A *social identity*:
   a.   is a kind of daydream
   b.   is firmly fixed in reality
   c.   typically has little to do with people's plans for action
   d.   our sense of who and what we are

6.   According to the text's discussion, *fashion*:
   a.   is reflection of cultural ambivalences
   b.   is as old a tradition as societies themselves
   c.   is synonymous with *style*
   d.   seldom changes

7.   Erving Goffman pointed out that "much of the activity during an encounter can be understood as an effort on everyone's part to get through the occasion and all the unanticipated and unintentional events that can cast participants in an undesirable light, without disrupting the relationships of participants." This illustrates what Goffman called:
   a.   ethnomethodology
   b.   face-work
   c.   the definition of the situation
   d.   the presentation of self

8. Three types of "currency" are involved in social exchanges. Which of the following is NOT one of these?
    a. material rewards
    b. intrinsic rewards
    c. identity support
    d. reciprocity

9. According to the text's discussion, *networks*:
    a. can only be understood from a macroapproach
    b. depend upon frequent contact
    c. are created through social interaction
    d. are unfamiliar in most people's lives

10. A collection of people who just happen to be in the same place at the same time defines a/an:
    a. social category
    b. aggregate
    c. social group
    d. reference group

11. Suppose we classify all people who are left-handed. This collection of left-handed people is a:
    a. social group
    b. reference group
    c. social category
    d. primary group

12. A number of people who feel a common identity and interact in a regular and structured way on the basis of shared norms and goals comprise a:
    a. social group
    b. social category
    c. reference group
    d. primary group

13.   Which of the following is an example of a primary group?
   a.   a division in the military
   b.   a retirement planning committee
   c.   International Business Machines (IBM)
   d.   the family

14.   John Jones is a member of the varsity squad on his high school football team; he and his teammates are "true to their school." For John and his fellow players, this affiliation best represents a/an:
   a.   out-group
   b.   in-group
   c.   triad
   d.   reference group

15.   John Jones and his teammates feel very competitive with the other high school football teams in their conference. For John and his fellows, these other teams best represent:
   a.   out-groups
   b.   in-groups
   c.   secondary groups
   d.   reference groups

16.   John Jones and the members of his 10th grade class are acquainted with each other, share the same social status, and are approximately the same age. John and his fellow students constitute a/an:
   a.   out-group
   b.   reference group
   c.   social category
   d.   peer group

17.   The smallest possible group is a/an:
   a.   triad
   b.   quatranary
   c.   dyad
   d.   social group

18. The _____ can suffer the loss of one member and still be a group, and creates the possibility of coalitions and exclusions.
    a. social group
    b. triad
    c. dyad
    d. reference group

19. When outside experts or skeptics raise questions about the wisdom of a group's decisions, the members of this group may unite in opposing and discrediting the new information. This process has been referred to as:
    a. "groupthink"
    b. a risky shift
    c. instrumental/expressive leadership
    d. formal thinking

20. J.A. Stoner hypothesized that groups may take a more daring course in decision making in comparison to decisions made individually. He coined the term _____ to describe this process.
    a. "groupthink"
    b. risky shift
    c. informal thinking
    d. expressive thinking

Answers

1. b: Ethnomethodology means "people rules," referring to the countless unspoken assumptions that add order and predictability to our interactions with other people. (Cultural Scripts and Ethnomethodology; pp. 200-201)

2. a: Defining the situation is a collective process but arriving at a collective definition may involve disagreement between the individuals involved. (Defining the Situation; p. 201)

3. a: Frontstage behavior occurs in public, while "backstage" behavior takes place in private. In public, most couples work to create the impression of a happy marriage, but privately, they may engage in considerable conflict. (Backstage and Frontstage; p. 201)

4. c: Goffman emphasized the social ploys all of us use but seldom

admit, that each of us has an image of how we want to be seen by others. Far from passively accepting the roles "society" writes for us, we actively work to present ourselves in a certain light: We engage in *impression management*. (The Presentation of Self; pp. 201; 203)

5.   d: A *social identity* is "our sense of who and what we are." Social identities are not simply daydreams; they are a major source of plans for action; and they are fragile. (Social Identities; p. 203)

6   a: Sociologist Fred Davis points out that fashion is a reflection of cultural ambivalences that create personal insecurities which may be resolved, at least temporarily, through fashion. Fashion is a relatively recent phenomenon that differs from style in that it (fashion) is constantly changing. (Looking the Part: Fashion and Fitness; p. 204)

7   b: When people interact, they all have a stake in the encounter. If one actor blows his or her part, the others' performances are spoiled. If one person loses face, the others are embarrassed. Hence, people tend to support one another's efforts at impression management: to *save face*. (Negotiations and "Face-Work"; pp. 205-206)

8.   d: Reciprocity is involved in social exchange, but people tend to gravitate toward the situations and relationships that offer material rewards, intrinsic satisfaction, and identity support. (Exchange and Reciprocity; pp. 206-207)

9.   c: Networks are webs of relationships that connect an individual to many other people and are created through social interaction, although they do not depend on frequent contact. They are a familiar part of our everyday lives. There are several approaches to studying networks, including a micro- and macroapproach.. (Networks: The Social Fabric; pp. 207-209

10.   b: "Group" is a multipurpose word. Sometimes, people use it to describe aggregates: a collection of people who just happen to be in the same place at the same time. (What Is A Group?; p. 210)

11.   c: A social category consists of individuals who are classified together because they share a certain characteristic. (What Is A Group?; p. 210)

12.   a: Social groups differ from haphazard collections of individuals in four ways: shared identity, regular interaction, social structure,

and dependency on consensus. (What Is A Group?; p. 210)

13.   d: Primary groups are small, warm associations based on ongoing, personal, intimate relationships. (Types of Groups; p. 211)

14.   b: In-groups are groups to which people feel that they belong; they command their loyalty and respect. (Types of Groups; pp. 213-214)

15.   a: Out-groups are those one feels opposed to or in competition with. (Types of Groups; pp. 213-214)

16.   d: Peer groups are informal, primary social groups whose members share the same social status and are usually the same age. (Types of Groups; p. 214)

17.   c: The dyad, or two-person group, is the smallest possible group. (The Importance of Group Size: Dyads and Triads; p. 215)

18.   b: The triad, or three-person group, differs from a dyad in these two important respects. (The Importance of Group Size: Dyads and Triads; p. 215)

19.   a: Irving Janis used the term "groupthink" to refer to situations where loyalty to the group may lead to some questionable decision making; after a decision has been made, members tend to withhold information or opinions. (Behavior in Groups; pp. 220-221)

20.   b: Stoner's research regarding the "risky shift" suggests that groups tend to reduce individual inhibitions and release a desire for adventure. (Behavior in Groups; p. 222)

CRITICAL THINKING

1.   In one of his many investigations, social psychologist Stanley Milgram asked a group of male graduate students in New York to participate in a simple experiment. The student was to get on a subway, pick out one passenger in the crowd, and ask that person to give him his/her seat. Milgram's students thought he was crazy: "A person could get killed that way." One student agreed to try it. To his great surprise, half of the people he approached actually gave him their seat without asking for an explanation. When Milgram tried it himself, he discovered that the most difficult part was *making the request*. Sociologist Harold Garfinkel asked his students to commit similar violations of folkways, such as attempting

to bargain for items in a department store or breaking the rules in a game of tic-tac-toe by erasing their opponent's first move. How would you feel about participating in one of these experiments? What does your own reaction tell you about the unconscious, habitual level of social structure? About the presentation of self?

2. Observing the conditions of exchange and reciprocity in social relationships can tell you a great deal about the expectations that we have for people's behavior. For example, consider the elaborate ritual that frequently accompanies *visiting another person's home*. The visitors might be expected to notice that their host/hostess' carpet has just been cleaned: "Oh, I can see that you just shampooed your rug; I'll just leave my shoes by the door." The host/hostess, trying to be polite, may say, "Oh, that's o.k., don't worry about it...come on in before you freeze." However, this comment may not be taken literally, because beneath this exterior, he/she really WANTS the guest to remove his/her shoes. The visitor is expected to sense this: "No, I really insist....I don't want to get your carpet dirty." The host/hostess may even *continue* the exchange at this point: "Really, it's alright...leave your shoes on...just come on in!" Finally, the "best" outcome is for the guest to remove his/her shoes.

    One may ask WHY this elaborate ritual is necessary; wouldn't it be simpler if the host/hostess merely *asked* the visitor to remove his/her shoes? Using the knowledge you have acquired from this chapter, think about the explanations for such rituals in human interactions.

WEB EXERCISE: Exploring the Dynamics of Leadership

The text points out that group structure has a significant impact on the way individuals act and even how they think. The leadership structure of any group is a very important component of how each member of that group will behave. Effective leadership--in formal organizations as well as in small groups--depends on a balance of expressive and instrumental, democratic or laissez faire and directive styles.

The following web sites will introduce you to various dimensions of leadership. By exploring these sites, you will become better acquainted with the importance of leadership in terms of group structure and social interaction:

http://www.opc.on.ca/pubs/facts/leadership/index.html

http://www.srg.co.uk/exhiblead.html

Chapter Seven

DEVIANCE AND SOCIAL CONTROL

OBJECTIVES

After reading Chapter Seven, you should be able to provide detailed responses to the following questions:

1.   What is deviance?
2.   How do societies determine what constitutes deviance and attempt to control deviant behavior, and what are the consequences for offenders?
3.   How do sociologists explain deviance? What are the major theories of deviance?
4.   What are the most common types of crime in American society?
5.   How does America's criminal justice system operate?

CHAPTER REVIEW

I.   What is deviance?

The chapter opens with a discussion of colonial Americans' views of alcohol consumption in order to illustrate the social dynamics of deviance. From a sociological perspective, *deviance* is a violation of social rules, occurring when someone breaches a society's or group's widely held values and norms. From an *absolutist perspective*, deviance lies in the act itself.

II.   How do societies determine what constitutes deviance and attempt to control deviant behavior, and what are the consequences for offenders?

A. Deviance is universal, since every society establishes rules and regulations, experiences violations of those rules, and in one way or another punishes offenders. On the other hand, what does or does not upset people--the *social* *definition* of deviance--is highly variable. Americans' attitudes toward consuming alcohol are analyzed through this sociological framework. It is pointed out that even *within* a society, the social definition of deviance varies according to the actor, the audience, and the situation; in short, beliefs about what is or is not deviant can and do change over time. The "where," "when," and "with whom" dimensions are examined through a discussion of drinking on college campuses.

B. *Social control* refers to any and all efforts to prevent and/or correct deviant behavior; the most powerful instrument of social control is socialization. To achieve control, all societies depend on *sanctions*, that is, on rewards for conforming behavior and punishments for deviant behavior. A broad distinction can be made between formal and informal social controls: *Informal social controls* are subtle, unofficial pressures to conform to society's norms and values. *Formal social controls* are institutionalized, codified, public mechanisms for preventing or correcting deviant behavior.

C. To understand and explain the social dynamics of deviance, many sociologists employ a perspective known as *labeling* . This perspective focuses on the meanings and interpretations people attach to different kinds of behavior and on the process of interaction between those who make and enforce the rules and those who get caught breaking the rules.

Before an act can be labeled as deviant and the people who are involved can be labeled as "outsiders," there must be a rule against it. *Moral entrepreneurs* are people (or groups) who make it their business to see that offenses are recognized and that offenders are treated as such.

Sociologists distinguish between *primary deviance*, or the initial violation of a social rule, and *secondary deviance*, or deviance that results from other people's reactions to the initial violations. A "deviant" label can create a master status--one that overrides all others.

Erich Goode identified six elements of deviant stereotyping--assumptions people tend to make about deviance and individuals they consider deviant: exaggeration, centrality, persistence, dichotomizing, homogeneity, and clustering.

An individual who has been labeled may be pushed into a *deviant career*-- that is, a lifestyle that includes habitual or permanent deviance; and this may draw that person into a *deviant subculture*--that is, a group that is distinguished from other members of society by deviant norms, values, and lifestyle.

The sequence of events from primary deviance to labeling and secondary deviance is not inevitable; many people successfully reject the label "deviant" through the process of *rationalization*. According to Sykes and Matza, rationalization displays five major techniques: denial of responsibility, denial of injury, denial of the victim, condemnation of the condemners, and appeal to higher loyalties.

The strengths of labeling theory are also its weaknesses: the social definition of deviance is arbitrary, and the theory fails to explain why people break social rules in the first place.

III.   How do sociologists explain deviance? What are the major theories of deviance?

A. How one explains deviance depends in part on which questions one asks. Biological and psychological theories attempt to answer the question of why certain individuals engage in certain forms of deviance; sociological theories address the social circumstances that permit and even promote deviance. From the sociologist's point of view, the basic flaw in biological and psychological theories of deviance is that they tend to assume that all the causes of deviance lie inside the individual--in his/her genes, brain chemistry, psyche, or personal experiences. Sociologists are primarily concerned with general patterns, not individual acts; with nomothetic rather than idiographic explanations.

B. Durkheim linked deviant behavior to a breakdown in the social order; he saw high rates of deviance as the result of *anomie*--a condition of "normlessness," or loss of accepted social rules within a society. The idea that crime and deviance are products of anomie dominated sociological thinking for many years.

C. Control theory can be seen as a modern effort to refine and expand Durkheim's theory. Hirschi argued that deviance is most likely to occur when the bond between the individual and society is weak or nonexistent. In analyzing delinquent behavior, he emphasized four controls: attachment to parents, the school, the peer group, and aspiration to conventional lines of action. The main critique of control theory is that it does not deal with motivation to break the law.

D. In a critique of Durkheim's theory of anomie and an extension of control theory, Robert Merton argued that our desires are *created* by the sociocultural system. Merton described five possible responses to the gap that can exist between culturally prescribed goals and socially structured opportunities: conformity, innovation, ritualism, retreatism, and rebellion. Merton's key point is that deviance is a product of the social system, not of abnormality within the individual. Cloward and Ohlin expanded on Merton's thinking with their notion of illegitimate opportunities.

E. Another challenge to the theory of deviance and anomie is the theory of *cultural transmission*; cultural transmission theory views deviance as the result of socialization to a subculture that applauds attitudes and behavior that the mainstream culture rejects. Sutherland theorized that individuals become delinquent or criminal through *differential association*: when they are exposed to more procriminal than anticriminal norms and values for long periods or when they generally find themselves in situations that reward criminal behavior. The major flaw in Sutherland's theory is that it does not explain why deviant subcultures emerge in the first place.

F. The *conflict perspective on deviance* is rooted in the work of Karl Marx. Conflict theory directs attention away from those who break the law toward those who *make* the law. From this perspective, the *reality* of law resides in particular definitions of what is right, wrong, moral, immoral, normal, and abnormal. According to conflict theory, the temperance movement was not only an attempt to ban drinking, but also an effort to retain power and privilege: Joseph Gusfield called such efforts a *symbolic crusade*. The text discusses the politics of prohibition in terms of a symbolic crusade. The changing legal definitions of rape also illustrate the role of power in defining what is and is not criminal.

IV. What are the most common types of crime in American society?

A. A *crime* is the violation of a norm that has been codified in a law and is backed by the power and authority of the state. Although deviance and crime often overlap, they are not synonymous. Crime can be divided into five basic types: violent and property crimes (or "common" crime), white-collar crime, corporate crime, organized crime, and crimes without victims. *Violent crimes*, like murder, rape, robbery, and assault, involve a direct confrontation between the criminal and the victim; *property crimes* include burglar, larceny, auto theft, and other "minor" crimes. *White-collar crime* refers to violations of the law committed by middle- and upper-middle-class people in the course of their business and social lives. Whereas white-collar crime consists of crimes against the corporation, *corporate crime* consists of crimes committed *by* the corporation, *on behalf* of the corporation. *Organized crime* involves organizations that exist primarily to provide, and profit from, illegal goods and services. *Crimes without victims* are activities that have been declared illegal because they offend public morals, not because they cause anyone direct harm.

B. By almost any measure, the United States is one of the most violent nations in the world; the crime rates are very high. Sociologists distinguish between the *absolute number of crimes* and the *crime rate*. Although the crime rate is declining, most Americans agree that the levels of violence and theft in our society are unacceptably high.

V. How does America's criminal justice system operate?

The criminal justice system is best described as a funnel. Only about 50 percent of all crimes are reported to the police, and only about half of these crimes are *cleared by arrest*. Less than half of those suspects who are arrested are tried and convicted, and only a small percentage of these people are sent to prison and complete their sentences. The main reason is that the police, the courts, and the prisons are given considerable discretion in applying sanctions. There are four main reasons for imposing criminal sanctions: retribution, incapacitation, deterrence, and rehabilitation. Decisions concerning crime and punishment may be based on practical or personal considerations, not the *letter of the law*. Whether the threat of punishment acts as a deterrent to crime is the subject of much debate, much of which sorts out on political grounds. There is ongoing debate over whether capital punishment acts as a deterrent and whether it is "cruel and unusual."

CONCEPT REVIEW

Match each of the following terms with the correct definition.

a.	innovators (p. 243	k.	corporate crime (p. 249)
b.	formal social controls (p. 235)	l.	conformists (p. 243)
		m.	deviance (p. 228)
c.	deviant subculture (p. 238)	n.	differential association (p. 243)
d.	crime (p. 246)		
e.	anomie (p. 240)	o.	informal social controls (p. 235)
f.	crime rate (p. 255)		
g.	ritualists (p. 243)	p.	labeling perspective (p. 236)
h.	white-collar crime (p. 247)	q.	deviant career (p. 238)
i.	social control (p. 235)	r.	sanctions (p. 235)
j.	moral entrepreneurs (p. 237)	s.	retreatists (p. 243)

t.   rebels (p. 243)
u.   organized crime (p. 251)
v.   absolute number of crimes (p. 255)
w.   deterrence (p. 261)
x.   primary deviance (p. 237)
y.   neutralization (p. 238)
z.   secondary deviance (p. 237)
aa.   "three-strikes" laws (p. 261)
bb.   crimes without victims (p. 252)
cc.   retribution (p. 260)
dd.   absolutist perspective (p. 255)
ee.   symbolic crusade (p. 244)
ff.   rehabilitation (p. 262)
gg.   incapacitation (p. 261)

1.___ A violation of a norm that is codified in a law and backed by the power and authority of the state.

2.___ Sutherland's term for the learning of criminal or violent behavior through exposure to predominantly procriminal norms and values or to situations that reward criminal behavior.

3.___ Unofficial pressures to conform to society's norms and values.

4.___ A condition of normlessness in a society.

5.___ Merton's term for the people who accept both the goals their culture holds out as desirable and the approved means.

6.___ Focuses on the process of interaction between those who make and enforce the rules and those who are identified as breaking the rules.

7.___ Crimes committed *by* corporations, *on behalf* of the corporations.

8.___ Efforts to prevent and/or correct deviant behavior.

9.___ Merton's term for people who reject both the culturally prescribed goals and the socially approved rules, and substitute new goals and new means of achieving them.

10.___ Merton's term for people who have given up on both the goals and the means for attaining them.

11.___ Social rewards for conforming behavior and punishments for deviant behavior.

12.___ The number of crimes per 100,000 population during a given time period.

13.___ Becker's term for people who make it their business to see that offenses are recognized and offenders treated as such.

14.___ The violation of social rules.

15.___ Institutionalized, codified, public mechanisms for preventing or correcting deviant behavior.

16.___ Merton's term for people who are determined to achieve conventional goals but are willing to use unconventional means of achieving them.

17. ___ Involves organizations that exist primarily to provide, and profit from, illegal goods and services.

18. ___ A life style that includes habitual or permanent deviance.

19. ___ Violations of the law committed by middle- and upper-middle-class people in the course of their business and social lives.

20. ___ Merton's term for people who are so compulsive about following social rules that they lose sight of the goals.

21. ___ A group that is distinguished from other members of society by deviant norms, values, and life style.

22. ___ The number of crimes committed during a given time period, often measured in terms of the number of crimes *known*.

23. ___ Deviance that results from other people's reactions to the initial violations.

24. ___ Using sentences to inhibit or prevent criminal activity.

25. ___ The process of rationalizing one's deviant behavior in ways that both relieve feelings of guilt and turn aside other people's expressions of disapproval.

26. ___ The initial violation of a social rule.

27. ___ Activities that have been declared illegal because they offend public morals, not because they cause anyone direct harm.

28. ___ An effort by members of a social class or ethnic group to preserve, defend, or enhance their position in relation to other groups in their society.

29. ___ Advocates of incapacitation support these laws, which target repeat offenders.

30. ___ According to this view, deviance lies in the act itself, which may be viewed as a violation of natural law or a transgression against God's commandments.

31. ___ An ancient approach to social control with the goal of restoring social balance by forcing criminals to pay back society for the crimes they have committed.

32. ___ Designed to protect society by confining criminals to prison or otherwise preventing them from committing additional crimes.

33. ___ An approach reflecting the view that the goal of imprisonment is not just to punish criminals but also to reform them and that in some sense, society promotes criminal activities through various forms of social inequality.

Answers

1.	d	12.	f	23.	z
2.	n	13.	j	24.	w
3.	o	14.	m	25.	y
4.	e	15.	b	26.	x
5.	l	16.	a	27.	bb
6.	p	17.	u	28.	ee
7.	k	18.	q	29.	aa
8.	i	19.	h	30.	dd
9.	t	20.	g	31.	cc
10.	s	21.	c	32.	gg
11.	r	22.	v	33.	ff

REVIEW QUESTIONS

1. According to the text, deviance:
   a. is not universal
   b. is a violation of the social rules
   c. elicits social approval
   d. remains consistent through time

2. From a/an *absolutist* perspective, deviance lies in:
   a. social definition
   b. specific labels
   c. the act itself
   d. collective judgments

3. Unofficial pressures to conform to society's norms and values are referred to as:
   a. deviant sanctions
   b. formal social controls
   c. gossip
   d. informal social controls

4.   Institutionalized, codified, public mechanisms for preventing or correcting deviant behavior are:
     a.   formal social controls
     b.   informal social controls
     c.   gossip
     d.   labels

5.   The temperance movement took a/an _____ position toward alcohol, similar to public attitudes toward illicit drugs today.
     a.   relative
     b.   absolute
     c.   subjective
     d.   labeling

6.   *Primary deviance* refers to:
     a.   the initial violation of a social rule
     b.   the most important kind of deviant behavior
     c.   deviance that results from other people's reactions to the initial violations
     d.   discredited deviance

7.   *Secondary deviance* refers to:
     a.   the initial violation of a social rule
     b.   deviant behavior that is less serious in comparison to primary deviance
     c.   discredited deviance
     d.   deviance that results from other people's reactions to the initial violations

8.   A lifestyle that includes habitual or permanent deviance is referred to as:
     a.   secondary deviance
     b.   primary deviance
     c.   a deviant career
     d.   a deviant subculture

9.   A group that is distinguished from other members of society by deviant norms, values, and lifestyle is referred to as a:
   a.   deviant subculture
   b.   deviant reference group
   c.   master status group
   d.   neutralized group

10.   Which of the following is NOT one of Sykes and Matza's techniques of neutralization?
   a.   denial of responsibility
   b.   condemnation of the condemners
   c.   appeal to higher loyalties
   d.   self-corruption

11.   Durkheim's term for the condition of "normlessness," or loss of accepted social rules within a society, is:
   a.   anomie
   b.   discontinuity
   c.   absent social control
   d.   cultural transmission

12.   The main critique of control theory is that it:
   a.   is unscientific
   b.   is unfounded
   c.   is incomplete
   d.   fails to explain secondary deviance

13.   Merton used the term *rebel* to describe people who:
   a.   pursue culturally approved goals by illegitimate means
   b.   abide by society's rules but lose sight of the goals
   c.   abandon culturally approved goals and legitimate means to achieve them
   d.   reject cultural values and norms, but substitute new goals and rules for action

14.　The top management of a corporation may encourage white-collar crime by setting impossibly high goals for middle management and blocking efforts to discuss methods of achieving those goals. Top management is encouraging:
a.　conformity
b.　ritualism
c.　innovation
d.　retreatism

15.　Which of the following sociologists emphasized the role of *differential association* in generating deviance?
a.　Robert Merton
b.　Richard Cloward
c.　Edwin Sutherland
d.　Travis Hirschi

16.　Conflict theory directs attention toward:
a.　people who break the law
b.　people who make the law
c.　lower-class people who are responsible for crime
d.　the members of the working class

17.　Whereas political movements seek to replace one form of government, a particular group of leaders, or the prevailing political ideology with another, *symbolic crusades* focus on:
a.　deviant behavior
b.　class conflict
c.　private ownership
d.　lifestyles and public morals

18.　Which of the following is NOT an example of white-collar crime?
a.　suppressing a study that shows workers in a paint factory are being exposed to high levels of toxic substances
b.　using intimidation (threats of sabotage, violence, etc.) to obtain a contract for garbage collection
c.　using bribery to obtain a contract for garbage collection
d.　embezzling money from a bank

19.   Crime itself can be divided into five basic types. Which of the following is NOT among the five?
    a.   conflict crime
    b.   common crime
    c.   white-collar crime
    d.   crimes without victims

20.   In the 1960s, many prisons were renamed "correctional facilities" and prison guards were given the new job title of "correction officer." These changes reflected the view that the goal of imprisonment should be:
    a.   punishment
    b.   parole
    c.   tethered probation
    d.   rehabilitation

Answers

1.   b: Sociologically, deviance is a violation of the social rules; it is universal, it elicits social disapproval, and definitions concerning deviance change substantially over time. (The Social Definition of Deviance; p. 228)

2.   c: From an absolutist perspective, deviance lies in the act itself rather than definition, labels, or collective judgments. (What is Deviance?; p. 228)

3.   d: Informal social controls are tightly woven into the fabric of everyday life and may even be overlooked. (Deviance and Social Control; p. 235)

4.   a: In modern societies, certain institutions and organizations specialize in social control, such as the police, the courts, and the prisons. (Deviance and Social Control; p. 235)

5.   b: The temperance movement illustrates an absolutist position because it was viewed as dangerous and addictive rather than relative to the user or subjectively determined through labeling. (The Social Definition of Deviance; p. 230)

6.   c: According to labeling theory, no act is deviant in and of itself; rather, deviance is an interactive process whereby certain behaviors are *defined* as deviant. (The Labeling Perspective; p. 237)

7.   a: Sociologists distinguish between primary and secondary deviance.

(The Labeling Perspective. 237)

8.   c: As Erving Goffman pointed out: "One response to [being labeled deviant] is to embrace it." This yields a deviant career. (The Labeling Perspective; p. 238)

9.   a: Becoming a member of a deviant subculture usually represents a completion of the break with conventional society. (The Labeling Perspective; p. 238)

10.   d: Many people successfully reject the label "deviant" through neutralization, consisting of denial of responsibility, denial of injury, denial of the victim, condemnation, and appeal to higher loyalties (The Labeling Perspective; p. 238).

11.   a: The idea that crime and deviance are products of anomie, or normlessness, dominated sociological thinking for many years. (Deviance and Anomie; p. 240)

12.   c: Attachment and aspirations may explain why people, especially young people, play by the rules; but what causes people to break the law? (Control Theory; p. 242)

13.   d: Anarchists are one example. Members of unconventional religious sects that require members to alter their life style radically are another. (Deviance and Social Structure; p. 243)

14.   c: In effect, the corporate heads are asking middle management to achieve accepted goals by illegal means. Note that they create an atmosphere that encourages innovation, while, at the same time, avoiding any personal responsibility for illegal activities. (Deviance and Social Structure; p. 243)

15.   c: Sutherland held that learning deviant values is as significant as learning deviant skills and that we learn values from our close associations. (Cultural Transmission; p. 243)

16.   b: As Richard Quinney argues, criminal law is a reflection of the interests and ideologies of the ruling class. (Conflict Theory; p. 244)

17.   d: Symbolic crusades focus on lifestyles and morals. (Theories of Deviance; p. 244)

18.   b: The use of physical intimidation is associated with organized crime. Note that the line between organized and white-collar crime is a fine one. (Crime and the Justice System; pp. 247-248).

19.   a: The five basic types of crime are: violent and property crimes (or "common" crime), white-collar crime, corporate crime, organized

crime, and crimes without victims. (Crime and the Justice System/Types of Crime; p. 246)

20.   d: In the 1960s, the goal of imprisonment was viewed as not just to punish criminals but to reform them; when crime rates began to rise in the 1970s, however, rehabilitation was declared a failure. (The Goals of the Justice System; p. 262)

CRITICAL THINKING

1.   As explained in this chapter, deviance is not an absolute. A behavior can be called deviant only when it violates the norms of some group. This suggests that definitions of deviance will change as societies evolve. What are some behaviors now considered acceptable that were formerly thought to be deviant? Are there any now considered deviant that were once considered acceptable? Is there a trend toward defining more behaviors as deviant or more as acceptable?

2.   The FBI classifies many white-collar crimes, such as embezzlement and anti-trust violations, as less serious than violent crimes and certain property crimes. Conflict theorists sometimes contend that this reflects a social bias against the poor and in favor of dominant social groups, who are more likely to commit white-collar crimes. Do you agree with this interpretation? Should white-collar crimes receive stiffer penalties? Should the penalties for violent crimes and property crimes be less severe? Why?

WEB EXERCISE: Capital Punishment: Pro and Con

The controversy involving capital punishment rages on with a seemingly equal proportion of advocates and critics. This exercise encourages you to explore the issues, both pro and con, concerning the death penalty, using a number of web sites on the Internet:

"Pro and Con On the Death Penalty":
http://speech.santafe.cc.fl.us/speech/deathpen.html

"Death Penalty Information Center":
http://www.essential.org/dpic

"Public Broadcasting's Pro-Con on the Death Penalty":
http:/www.pbs.org/wgbh/pages/frontline/angel/procon/index.html

PART THREE

SOCIAL INEQUALITY

Chapter Eight

SOCIAL STRATIFICATION

OBJECTIVES

After reading Chapter Eight, you should be able to provide detailed responses to the following questions:

1. What is social stratification?
2. How do sociologists explain stratification?
3. How have patterns of social stratification changed over the past three decades?
4. How widespread is poverty in the United States?
5. What are the causes and consequences of global stratification?

CHAPTER REVIEW

I.   What is social stratification?

The term *social stratification* refers to the division of society into layers (or strata), whose occupants have unequal access to social opportunities and rewards.

Status refers to a person's position in the system of stratification. A *social class* is a grouping of individuals who occupy similar statuses or positions in the social hierarchy, and therefore share similar political and economic interests.

Status inconsistency occurs when one marker of social standing is out of sync with the others.

There are two basic forms of social stratification: in a *closed system*, a person's position in the social hierarchy is ascribed; in an *open system*, status is achieved.

Social mobility refers to movement up or down the socioeconomic ladder. Much of the mobility in the United States is the result of structural change, not individual success stories. *Structural mobility* occurs when technological innovations, urbanization, and other events alter the number and kinds of occupations available in a society.

II.   What are the major theories of stratification?

The text considers three theories of social stratification:

A.   Functionalists view stratification as an inevitable part of social life. If a society is to motivate talented people to fill roles that require long and difficult training and entail unpleasant work, it must offer these people special rewards. Underlying the functionalist view is the ideal of *meritocracy*, in which positions in society are distributed solely on the basis of merit.

B.   Karl Marx was an economic determinist who traced social stratification to the *means of production*. Throughout recorded history, Marx argued, societies have been divided into a ruling class, which controls the means of production, and an oppressed class, which has lost control of the products of its labor. The ruling class is in a position not only to exploit the laboring class, but also to dominate the political, social, and intellectual life of that society. As the mode of production changes, the composition of these classes also changes. In feudal societies, the ruling class was composed of landowners, and the oppressed class of serfs; in an industrial, capitalist society, the ruling class is the bourgeoisie (the owners of industry), and the oppressed class is the proletariat (propertyless workers). Marx held that industrial capitalism would inevitably lead to revolution and the creation of a workers' socialist state. For the first time in history, the majority of the population would control the means of production. Class distinctions would eventually disappear.

C.   Max Weber saw social stratification as multidimensional. An individual or group's position in society depends not only on wealth, but also on power and prestige. By wealth, Weber meant rights over economic resources and decisions as well as ownership of property. Power is the ability to achieve one's goals, despite opposition. Prestige is a social honor and esteem. The three do not necessarily go together. An artist may enjoy high esteem but have little wealth and no formal political power, for example. Weber did not deny the role of economics in social stratification, but argued that prestige and power are also important.

III.   Social Stratification in the United States

Americans rank one another into social classes according to a multitude of different criteria. In studying the American class structure, sociologists look at both objective criteria (education, income, etc.) and subjective criteria (how individuals rank themselves or other members of their communities). Dennis Gilbert divides American society into six social classes: *upper (capitalist), upper-middle, middle, working, working poor,* and *lower.*

In the last two decades, the distribution of wealth and income in the U.S. changed dramatically: The rich got richer, the poor got poorer, and the dream of a better life dimmed for the working and middle classes. The wealthiest fifth of the population earns more than ten times as much as the poorest fifth and the income gap between the rich and the poor has widened. But the most significant change in recent decades has been the declining fortunes of the working and middle classes. Inequality in wealth is even more pronounced than inequality in income.   Looking at net worth (assets minus debts), Gilbert identifies three groups: *the nearly propertyless class, the "nest-egg" class,* and *the investor class.*

Much of the wealth in America today is "new wealth"-- the Fortune 400 list tends to support the functionalist view that our economy is in large part a meritocracy in which fortunes are earned. Not only have the rich gotten richer, but more Americans are wealthy.

During the first part of the twentieth century, the middle-class expanded steadily, but during the past twenty-five or thirty years, opportunities to "get ahead" have dwindled and the middle class is shrinking. For most people, the American dream of upward mobility has not come true.

From the end of World War II in 1945 to about 1975, the United States enjoyed "shared prosperity," but beginning in 1975, Americans' fortunes took a "great U-turn." The gap between the rich and poor increased and the working and middle classes lost ground. This shift from shared prosperity to growing inequality coincided with changes in the structure of the economy: *Deindustrialization*--the shift from an economy based on manufacturing to one based on information and service--was fostered by *globalization* and *technology.*

As a result of these changes, the U.S. economy is in better shape, but most workers are not.

IV.   How widespread is poverty in America?

As a result of deindustrialization, the poor are poorer than they were 20 years ago. Between 1974 and 1994, the "poverty gap"--the amount of money the average poor family would need to rise above the poverty level--increased by 16 percent for families. The official *poverty line* is based on the federal government's estimate of a minimal budget for families of different sizes; this poverty line is the subject of much debate. There are many myths about the poor. The poor population is actually quite diverse. Although the risk of poverty is higher for minorities, the most numerous among the poor are non-Hispanic whites. Half the poor are either too old or too young to work. The majority of poor people live in suburbs, small towns, or rural areas. The majority of the poor are either married or living alone or with nonrelatives. Only 40 percent of the poor collect cash welfare benefits. Federal programs for the poor constitute only about 14 percent of the total federal budget. Most welfare programs are designed to sustain the poor rather than to lift them out of poverty.

One of the changes in the poor population in recent years is age: While the proportion of elderly Americans living in poverty has dropped, the proportion of poor children has climbed. A second trend is growth in the ranks of the working poor: People who work do not earn enough to keep themselves and their families out of poverty. Although most Americans supported government efforts to help the poor during the booming 1960s economy, the public is less sympathetic today and more likely to see the poor--especially welfare mothers--as undeserving.

The chronic, severe poverty in the nation's inner city black ghettos is the subject of ongoing debate. Whereas popular explanations invoke a "culture of poverty," Wilson holds that the ghetto poor are victims of the combined effects of deindustrialization and social isolation. Jencks holds that ghetto poverty is a variable phenomenon with many different causes.

Most researchers trace homelessness to a decline in low-skill jobs, a shortage of low-cost housing, cutbacks in social welfare programs, and social isolation. A number of factors have contributed to the increase in homelessness in recent decades, including a reduced demand for low-skilled workers, cutbacks in virtually all assistance programs for the poor, cutbacks in subsidies for the disabled, a decrease in the supply of low-income housing, and the arrival of crack-cocaine in the mid-1980s. Whatever the explanation may be, the consequences of poverty include shorter lifespans and generally poor health, as well as greater vulnerability to economic swings.

V.   What are the causes and consequences of global stratification?

The global system of stratification can be traced to the period of European colonization. Global stratification persists because of uneven development (economic diversification in rich nations, specialization in poor nations), control of technology by rich nations, and demography (ever-increasing dependent populations in poor nations). Today, the United States is unquestionably an "upper-class nation," but competition from "middle class" nations is increasing.

CONCEPT REVIEW

Match each of the following terms with the correct definition.

a.	prestige (p. 281)	i.	social mobility (p. 276)
b.	structural mobility (p. 277)	j.	closed system (p. 275)
c.	wealth (p. 285)	k.	power (p. 281)
d.	poverty line (p. 291)	l.	deindustrialization (p. 298)
e.	open system (p. 276)		
f.	meritocracy (p. 278)	m.	status (p. 274)
g.	social stratification (p. 274)	n.	status inconsistency (p. 274)
h.	social class (p. 274)		

1.___ Rights over socially desirable objects as well as ownership of the objects themselves.

2.___ A form of social stratification in which a person's position in the social hierarchy is ascribed.

3.___ A grouping of individuals who occupy similar statuses or positions in the social hierarchy, and therefore share similar political and economic interests.

4.___ Social standing--the degree of respect and/or esteem that a person receives.

5.___ Movement up or down the socioeconomic ladder in society.

6.___ The ability of an individual or group of people to realize their own will in a communal action even against the resistance of others who are participating in that action.

7.___ Changes in social position that occur because technological innovations, urbanization, economic booms or busts, wars, or other events have altered the number and kinds of occupations available in a society.

8.___ The federal government's estimate of a minimum budget for families of different sizes.

9.___ The division of society into layers whose occupants have unequal access to social opportunities and rewards.

10.___ A system in which social rewards are distributed on the basis of achievement.

11.___ A form of social stratification in which status is achieved.

12.___ Occurs when one marker of social standing is out of sync with the others.

13.___ A person's position in the system of stratification.

14.___ A decline in the portion of the economy that is devoted to manufacturing goods as opposed to providing services.

Answers

1.	c		6.	k		11.	e
2.	j		7.	b		12.	n
3.	h		8.	d		13.	m
4.	a		9.	g		14.	l
5.	i		10.	f			

REVIEW QUESTIONS

1. The division of society into layers is termed:
   a. social stratification
   b. status inconsistency
   c. status defects
   d. life chance matrix

2. _____ refers to a person's position in the system of stratification.
   a. Role
   b. Status
   c. Location
   d. Rank

3. Which of the following statements is *false*?
   a. Most societies can be characterized as having either closed or open social systems.
   b. In a closed social system, status is ascribed on the basis of characteristics over which the individual has little or no control.
   c. In an open social system, social status is achieved through personal talent and effort.
   d. In a closed social system, opportunities for social mobility are severely limited.

4. The term *working poor* refers to people who:
   a. are collecting welfare and working at the same time
   b. work but do not earn enough to support themselves and their dependents
   c. earn their livings through illegal jobs
   d. have lost their jobs and are temporarily poor

5. Sociologists use the term *wealth* to refer to:
   a. income
   b. property
   c. the things people own
   d. privilege

6. Sociologists use the term *income* to refer to:
   a. property
   b. privilege
   c. status
   d. the money people earn

7.   According to the text's discussion of the shrinking middle class:
  m.   during the 1950s and 1960s, the middle class began to shrink
  n.   during the past twenty-five or thirty years, opportunities to "get ahead" have broadened and expanded
  o.   the American dream of upward mobility is alive and well today
  p.   none of the above

8.   Two forces fostered deindustrialization, which are
  a.   recession and globalization
  b.   depression and technology
  c.   globalization and technology
  d.   postindustrial decline and cybernetics

9.   According to the text's discussion of the poor in America:
  a.   the great majority of the poor in America are African American and Latino
  b.   there are very few children in poverty
  c.   the average poor person is a "welfare freeloader"
  d.   poverty tends to be more severe in big cities

10.   University of Chicago sociologist William Julius Wilson argues that:
  a.   ghetto poverty is due to a "culture of poverty"
  b.   deindustrialization and social isolation are key factors in the rise of ghetto poverty
  c.   the term "underclass" is appropriately synonymous with the *undeserving* poor
  d.   all of the above

11.   Sociologist Christopher Jencks:
  a.   agrees with Wilson about the underclass
  b.   believes that the underclass exists, but disagrees with Wilson
  c.   argues that we perpetuate class and racial stereotypes
  d.   believes that problems must be lumped together to get at the explanation for ghetto poverty

12. The number of homeless persons in the U.S. is best estimated by which of the following parameters:
   a. 1 to 2 thousand
   b. 250,000 to 3 million or more
   c. unknown
   d. 20 million

13. The largest group of homeless persons is:
   a. single males aged 21-64
   b. women of all ages
   c. children under age 16
   d. elderly males over age 65

14. Which of the following is NOT one of the factors that has contributed to the increase in homelessness in recent years?
   a. changes in the structure of the economy
   b. a decrease in welfare funding
   c. alienation
   d. cutbacks in subsidies for the disabled

15. Studies of the economy indicate that people who are now in their twenties and thirties cannot expect their income to grow at the rate that their parents' generation experienced. Buying houses and supporting families become more and more difficult. This is an example of _____ mobility.
   a. upward
   b. downward
   c. lateral
   d. structural

16. According to Karl Marx, the _____ would eventually unite and overthrow the system that held them back.
   a. bourgeoisie
   b. proletariat
   c. landed aristocracy
   d. feudal lords

17.   Weber used the term *prestige* to refer to:
        a.   conspicuous consumption
        b.   social status
        c.   rights over property
        d.   social standing and esteem received from others

18.   Which of the following statements reflects the functionalist view of social stratification?
        a.   Supreme Court justices obtain their positions because of their upper-class backgrounds.
        b.   Schoolteachers have low salaries because they often come from a lower-middle-class background.
        c.   Physicians have high incomes because medical schools limit the number of admissions so that doctors are scarce.
        d.   Physicians have high incomes because their work requires long training, and because what they do is very important--a matter of life and death.

19.   One of the major reasons for the global system of stratification that exists among nations today is that:
        a.   industrial nations still control most of the natural resources in Third World nations
        b.   Third World nations lack the natural resources for industrialization
        c.   industrial nations control much of the technology of production and distribution
        d.   Third World nations have become too economically diversified

20.   According to the text's discussion of poverty in Russia (*A Global View*):
        a.   poverty has existed in Russia since the beginning of that nation
        b.   officially, poverty did not exist in Russia during the Soviet period
        c.   since the Communists were overthrown in 1991, the poverty rate in Russia has declined sharply
        d.   Russia's new market economy has produced considerable wealth and prosperity

Answers

1. a: Status inconsistency relates to social stratification but this is not its definition; sociologists do not discuss "status defects," and nothing has been written about a "life chance matrix" (What Is Social Stratification?; p. 274)

2. b: Location is a general description; a role refers to social expectations for behavior; rank is usually used in referring to a person's level of seniority or degree of supervisory authority, as in the military. (What Is Social Stratification?; p. 274)

3. a: Closed and open social systems are ideal types; most societies contain at least some elements of both types of systems. (Open and Closed Social Systems; pp. 275-276)

4. b: This term refers to people who want to work and do work, but whose skills and opportunities confine them to marginal jobs. (The American Class System; p. 283)

5. c: Wealth includes assets like stocks and bonds, and various consumer durables. (The Changing Distribution of Wealth and Income in the United States; p. 285)

6. d: A person may draw a high salary but spend everything he/she earns and so has little wealth. (The Changing Distribution of Wealth and Income in the United States; p. 285)

7. d: During the 1950s and 1960s, the middle class expanded steadily; during the past twenty-five or thirty years, opportunities to "get ahead" have dwindled; a number of signs show that the American dream of upward mobility is withering. (Social Stratification in the United States; pp. 286-288)

8. c: Two forces fostered deindustrialization: globalization and technology. (Social Stratification in the United States; p. 289)

9. d: The great majority of the poor (two-thirds) are white; many are children; female heads of households stand a much greater risk of being poor; although poverty is not exclusively an urban phenomenon, poverty tends to be more severe in big cities; and contrary to popular stereotypes, the average poor person is NOT a welfare freeloader. (Poverty in America; pp. 291-194)

10. b: Wilson argues that the "underclass" exists, but that it is not interchangeable with the "undeserving poor"--the latter is a popular stereotype; deindustrialization, social isolation, and the

combination of joblessness and social isolation set the ghetto poor apart. (The Ghetto Poor; pp. 297-299)

11.   c: Jencks disagrees with Wilson, arguing that a special category of ghetto poor may not even exist; he argues that in assuming that problems related to poverty are all interlinked, we perpetuate class and racial stereotypes; the belief that the problems of the inner-city poor are pervasive and self-perpetuating becomes an excuse for inaction. (The Ghetto Poor; p. 299)

12.   b: The exact number of homeless persons is difficult to determine. Current estimates indicate that the number is between 250,000 and 3 million or more. (The Homeless; p. 300)

13.   a: The proportion of homeless women is smaller but growing; there are children in poverty whose mothers are unmarried and destitute, but not a large number in comparison with men; and relatively few males age 65 and older are homeless. (The Homeless; p. 300)

14.   c: While homeless people are surely alienated, it was not alienation that led to their becoming homeless; the text cites changes in the structure of the economy, cutbacks in welfare programs, cutbacks in subsidies for the disabled, and decreases in the supply of low-income housing. (The Homeless; pp. 300-301)

15.   d: Structural mobility refers to changes in the standard of living that result from alterations in the economy, not individual tenacity or fortune; therefore, youthful members of the shrinking middle class may not be able to achieve what their parents did. (What is Social Stratification?; p. 277)

16.   b: Marx predicted that capitalism would eventually reach a point where its own advances could no longer be contained in a system where a relatively small number of people owned and controlled the means of production; like the bourgeoisie before them, the proletarian workers would unite to overthrow the system that held them back. (Theories of Social Stratification; p. 279)

17.   d: Weber emphasized that individuals who are neither wealthy nor powerful may still enjoy high regard in their society; saints and artists are examples. (Theories of Social Stratification; p. 281)

18.   d: All of the other answers reflect the conflict view of social stratification, which holds that those in power preserve their positions by limiting access to important and lucrative positions.

(Theories of Social Stratification; p. 278)

19.   c: Some Third World Nations are rich in natural resources (such as oil); in general, Third World nations tend to be economically specialized, not diversified. A major obstacle for these nations is dependence on imported technology (including the technology of management in some cases). (Global Stratification; pp. 304-305)

20.   b: Officially, poverty did not exist in Russia during the Soviet Period, but since the communists were overthrown in 1991, the poverty rate in Russia has tripled. Russia's new market economy has pushed increasing numbers into poverty. (Box/A Global View: Poverty in Russia: Before and After the Anti-Communist Revolution; pp. 306-307)

CRITICAL THINKING

1.   Our society has been described as a *meritocracy*, in which people's social positions are determined *solely* by their own accomplishments. According to this view, ascribed characteristics have no role in determining a person's position in the stratification hierarchy. How do you react to this point of view? In what ways would American society have to change in order to make it a true meritocracy? Would these changes be desirable? Why?

2.   Assume that everyone in our society received the same income regardless of their background, education, skills, or occupation. What problems would this create? Would it be difficult to recruit people for certain jobs? Would our stratification system disappear? In general, would the effects of such a step be more positive or negative?

WEB EXERCISE: Learning More About Poverty and Homelessness

A commonly asked question is: "Other than teaching in colleges and universities, what do sociologists DO?" In fact, there are a wide variety of career opportunities for sociologists, and one of these outlets involves working as a *demographer* for the U.S. Bureau of the Census.

The Census Bureau has its own web site:

http://www.census.gov
One interesting location within this site relates directly to poverty:

http://www.census.gov/hhes/www/poverty/html

The contents of this site will permit you to explore current statistics on poverty in the United States.

Another government organization that is related to poverty and welfare is the Department of Health and Human Services. The DHHS has a very interesting web site on *homelessness* that will allow you to explore this problem in considerable detail:

http://aspe.os.dhhs.gov/progsys/homeless

Chapter Nine

RACIAL AND ETHNIC STRATIFICATION

OBJECTIVES

After reading Chapter Nine, you should be able to provide detailed responses to the following questions:

1.   What are the social definitions of race, ethnicity, and minority group?
2.   How do patterns of intergroup relations vary across cultures and over time?
3.   What are the major patterns of racial and ethnic relations in the United States?
4.   What are the explanations for racial inequality?
5.   How did the civil rights movement begin, and where did it lead?
6.   What is the extent of racial and ethnic inequality in the United States today?

CHAPTER REVIEW

I.   What are the sociological definitions of race, ethnic group, and minority group?

The definitions of race, ethnic group, and minority group are not as straightforward as one might expect, but reflect changing social perceptions.

From a sociological perspective, a *race* is a category of people who see themselves and are seen by others as different because of characteristics that are assumed to be innate and biologically inherited. The concept of race is usually found in association with *racism*: the belief that another group is innately inferior to one's own group.

An ethnic group is a category of people who see themselves and are seen by others as set apart because of their cultural heritage.

Louis Wirth defined a *minority group* as a category of people who, because of their physical or cultural characteristics, are singled out from others in the society in which they live for differential and unequal treatment, and who therefore regard themselves as objects of collective discrimination. "Minority group" is a sociological, not a statistical, concept; it does not depend primarily on numbers. In Wirth's definition, four points emerge: minority group members are disadvantaged; they are held in low esteem; their membership is involuntary; and they are conscious of being a *people apart*.

The existence of minority groups implies the existence of a *majority group* that has gained the upper hand in society and guards its power and privilege, excluding outsiders from its ranks.

II.   How do patterns of intergroup relations vary across cultures and over time?

Patterns of intergroup relations can be seen as a continuum, ranging from *amalgamation* (blending) to *assimilation* (absorption of minority groups into the majority's culture and social institutions), *pluralism* (the coexistence of different racial and ethnic groups, whether egalitarian or not), *exploitation* (the majority using minorities for its own benefit), and *ethnic struggle* (from hate crimes to civil war and *genocide*). As reflected in *apartheid*, the particular pattern of racial and ethnic relations in a society reflects its unique history.

Assimilation takes different forms: cultural, structural, and primary.

Advocates of *multiculturalism* hold the view that there is strength in cultural diversity.

Exploitation takes many forms: *colonization, segregation, and slavery.*

III.   What are the major patterns of racial and ethnic relations in the United States?

Each chapter of U.S. history has produced its own patterns of intergroup relations; relations among races and ethnic groups have taken many different forms, from peaceful coexistence to genocide.

A. The *settlement* phase established an Anglo-Saxon, Protestant blueprint for the nation; non-British settlers were admitted reluctantly, out of economic necessity.

B. The *expansion* phase began after the Revolution, when the colonial population began to grow and to compete with Native Americans for land. One by one, Native American tribes were forced to leave their ancestral lands or die. By 1890, Native Americans had been reduced to colonial status. The expansion phase also included the conquest of the Southwest and its Mexican-American inhabitants in 1846.

C. The *agricultural development* of the South laid the foundation for a third phase in the nation's racial and ethnic history: black slavery. Slavery was institutionalized because it was economically profitable; because racist beliefs rationalized the denial of freedom to blacks; and because Africans were visible and far from home (making escape difficult). Although slavery was outlawed in 1863, the *Jim Crow* laws of the post-Reconstruction years reestablished black servitude.

D. The *industrial expansion* in the North during the post-Civil War years led to the fourth phase of our ethnic history, the waves of immigrants from northern and later eastern and southern Europe. Immigrants supplied much of the labor for the industrialization of America.

E. *Ghettos* are a comparatively recent social creation. Before 1900, both black and white people in northern cities lived, studied, and worked side by side; African Americans certainly did not enjoy equal opportunities, but the two racial groups lived in the same social worlds and interacted regularly; by 1940, most urban African Americans lived in all or mostly black neighborhoods; during the second half of the century, government policies had the unintended consequence of reinforcing residential segregation; today, one-third of African Americans live in large, run-down, crime-ridden, densely populated urban neighborhoods that show no signs of recovery.

IV.   What are the explanations for racial inequality?

Several theories of racial inequality have been advanced. One emphasizes biological differences; another, prejudice and discrimination; and a third stresses institutionalized racism.

A. Echoing Social Darwinists, a small number of scientists have argued that racial inequality is the result of hereditary differences.   One area of controversy is IQ test scores. The average score for blacks is lower than for whites. But, is this the result of hereditary differences or cultural bias in the tests? The most recent controversy over race and IQ was sparked by the publication of *The Bell Curve* by Richard Herrnstein and Charles Murray. These authors cite evidence that intelligence is in large part inherited and therefore fixed and immutable; they apply this argument to group differences, including the observation that there are biological explanations for intelligence differences between majority and minority groups. This research has become a magnet for opposing views: A large body of evidence refutes the idea that group differences in intelligence are hereditary. And, there is little evidence that IQ or other test scores predict future success. Research supports the view that an ethnic or racial group's position in society has a significant impact on measurements of intelligence, rather than the essence of the Herrnstein-Murray hypothesis.

B. Others attribute racial inequality to continuing prejudice and discrimination. *Prejudice* is an unfavorable attitude toward members of a group, based on stereotypes of that group; *discrimination* is the denial of rights and respect to individuals because they are members of a group, informal agreements to exclude them, or avoidance of intimate relationships. Whether or not discrimination continues depends in large part on whether it is profitable or costly. Prejudice can function as a self-fulfilling prophecy. If people are seen as inferior, they may be denied education and employment, and the fact that they therefore lack skills and jobs may then be cited as evidence of their alleged inferiority.

C. A third theory holds that once inequality has become part of the social structure, it develops a life of its own and persists even though prejudice and deliberate discrimination decline. This is the theory of *institutionalized racism*. Racial inequality in the United States today is an unintended consequence of accepted practices that seem to have no relationship to discrimination. The banking practice of red lining neighborhoods that are high risks for housing loans, for example, has the unintended consequence of denying mortgages to minorities.

The debate over *race versus class* centers around the question of whether racism causes inequality or whether inequality promotes racism. Sociologist William Julius Wilson argues that class has become more important than race in determining the life chances of African Americans; he maintains that the extreme poverty in black ghettos is not so much the result of prejudice and discrimination as of structural changes in urban economies. The result, says Wilson, is a new kind of poverty--and new prejudices. Still, Wilson also maintains that poverty (or class) is as much a *cause* as a consequence of prejudice.

Other sociologists believe that racial prejudice continues to affect black Americans of all social classes.

V.   How did the civil rights movement begin and where did it lead?

In 1954, the Supreme Court decision in *Brown v. Board of Education* overturned the *separate but equal* doctrine which had supported segregation by law. The civil rights movement, which began with the bus boycott in Montgomery, Alabama in 1956 and culminated in the March on Washington in 1963, prompted Congress to pass the Civil Rights and Voting Rights acts. The strategy of nonviolent protest provided a model for other protest movements of the 1960s and 1970s. In many ways, combating *de facto* segregation (unofficial discrimination) in the North proved as difficult as fighting *de jure* segregation in the South. Busing children to integrate schools and *affirmative action* programs were, and still are, controversial. But there is little evidence of the white backlash many observers anticipated. In recent years, however, programs to assist minorities have been cut back and enforcement of civil rights has been relaxed somewhat.

VI.   What is the extent of racial and ethnic inequality in the United States today?

African Americans have experienced substantial improvement with respect to equality since the days before the civil rights movement. On the other hand, they are far from achieving equality with white Americans.

Latinos are a diverse group (Mexican Americans, Puerto Ricans, and Cuban Americans) whose present circumstances reflect the conditions under which they lived upon arriving in this country. In socioeconomic terms, Latinos are among the most disadvantaged groups in American society.

Native Americans (American Indians, Aleuts, and Eskimos) are among the poorest of the poor. Although some Asian Americans and Pacific Islanders have achieved the American dream, their reputation as a "model minority" is a mixed blessing: this stereotype conceals the fact that many Asian Americans are struggling to survive; in the final analysis, Asian Americans continue to be seen as "not quite American."

CONCEPT REVIEW

Match each of the following terms with the correct definition.

a.   ethnic group (p. 316)
b.   segregation (p. 323)
c.   affirmative action (p. 342)
d.   genocide (p. 327)
e.   majority group (p. 319)
f.   nativism (p. 329)
g.   race (p. 316)
h.   prejudice (p. 336)
i.   minority group (p. 317)

j.   institutionalized racism
      (p. 339)
k.   assimilation (p. 321)
l.   stereotype (p. 336)
m.   racism (p. 316)
n.   discrimination (p. 336)
o.   slavery (p. 322)
p.   pluralism (p. 321)
q.   amalgamation (p. 321)
r.   multiculturalism (p. 322)

1.___   The intentional mass murder of a racial or ethnic group.
2.___   Laws or customs that impose physical and social separation on racial or ethnic minorities, denying members of these groups certain rights and opportunities.
3.___   A category of people who see themselves and are seen by others as different because of characteristics that are assumed to be innate and biologically inherited.
4.___   A category of people who see themselves and are seen by others as set apart because of their cultural heritage.
5.___   A category of people who have gained a dominant position in society and guard their power and privilege, excluding outsiders from their ranks.
6.___   The denial of opportunities and social esteem to individuals because they are members of a devalued group or category.
7.___   Established social patterns that have the unintended consequence of limiting the opportunities of certain social groups.
8.___   A category of people whose members are disadvantaged, held in low esteem, involuntarily excluded from valued social positions, and conscious of being a *people apart*.
9.___   Refers to the protection of majority institutions and privileges from immigrant influences.
10.___   An over generalization about a group and its members that goes beyond existing evidence.

11.___ Programs designed to open educational and job opportunities to minorities.

12.___ An unfavorable and rigid opinion of members of a social group or category.

13.___ Occurs when ethnic and racial minorities are absorbed by the dominant culture and differences are forgotten and destroyed.

14.___ The belief that a group which is considered a racial group is innately inferior.

15.___ Its advocates hold the view that there is strength in diversity; that people should respect cultural differences rather than cultural sameness.

16.___ A pattern of intergroup relations in which ethnic and racial groups maintain their own language, religion, and customs, and socialize mainly among themselves.

17.___ A practice in which members of a group are kidnaped, held captive, forced to work for their captors, and treated as property.

18.___ The melting pot; a society in which different ethnic and racial groups intermingle, producing an entirely new and distinctive genetic and cultural blend.

Answers

1.	d	7.	j	13.	m
2.	b	8.	i	14.	k
3.	g	9.	f	15.	r
4.	a	10.	l	16.	p
5.	e	11.	c	17.	o
6.	n	12.	h	18.	q

REVIEW QUESTIONS

1. Suppose that a group of people see themselves and are seen by others as different because of characteristics that are assumed to be innate and biologically inherited. These people constitute a/an:
    a. ethnic group
    b. race
    c. authoritarian category
    d. inferiority complex

2. Suppose that a group of people see themselves and are seen by others as set apart because of their cultural heritage. These people constitute a/an:
    a. ethnic group
    b. race
    c. authoritarian category
    d. inferiority complex

3. Which of the following groups does not qualify as a minority group in the United States?
    a. African Americans
    b. the poor
    c. women
    d. homosexuals

4. Which of the following is NOT one of the key points in Wirth's definition of a minority group?
    a. disadvantage
    b. low esteem
    c. similar external characteristics
    d. involuntary membership

5. _____ has gained the upper hand in society and guards its power and privilege, excluding outsiders from its ranks.
    a. A minority group
    b. A racial emphasis group
    c. Apartheid
    d. A majority group

6.   Colonial Brazil provided an example of:
        a.   amalgamation
        b.   cultural pluralism
        c.   Anglo-conformity
        d.   genocide

7.   A man brags to his small-town relatives about the ethnic diversity of his neighborhood in the city. He is impressed by how quickly the Asian children in his daughter's school learn English. He has hired Jamaicans and Hondurans in his business. But, he is deeply distressed when his son announces his engagement to a Puerto Rican woman. What level of assimilation has this man NOT accepted?
        a.   cultural
        b.   structural
        c.   primary
        d.   none of the above

8.   Most major cities in the United States have a Chinatown, a Little Italy, and a Spanish quarter. These ethnic enclaves illustrate:
        a.   cultural assimilation
        b.   structural assimilation
        c.   primary assimilation
        d.   pluralism

9.   A sociologist gives a lecture about the substantial strength of cultural diversity and how Americans should respect cultural differences. This person is an advocate of:
        a.   multiculturalism
        b.   cultural assimilation
        c.   primary assimilation
        d.   structural assimilation

10.   Which of the following is NOT one of the patterns of intergroup relations discussed in the text?
        a.   amalgamation
        b.   assimilation
        c.   reification
        d.   exploitation

11.   In the language of the Afrikaners, *apartheid* means:
a.   "racial hatred"
b.   "separate development"
c.   "company town"
d.   "bossdom"

12.   The incorporation of the Southwest and its Hispanic population into the United States was part of which phase of U.S. ethnic history?
a.   settlement
b.   expansion
c.   agricultural development
d.   industrial development

13.   The text points out that Richard Herrnstein and Charles Murray's *The Bell Curve* was a magnet for opposing views. Critics pointed out that
a.   intelligence is far more complex, variable and changeable than a single test score suggests.
b.   a large body of evidence refutes the idea that group differences in intelligence are hereditary.
c.   there is little evidence that IQ or other test scores predict future success.
d.   all of the above

14.   The beliefs that all Asians are smart; that all Jewish people are cheap; that all African Americans are lazy; and that all Italians are part of the Mafia reflect:
a.   discrimination
b.   stereotypes
c.   cultural pluralism
d.   assimilation

15.   Which of the following is an example of institutionalized racism?
a.   the bombing of a black church in Birmingham, Alabama
b.   opposition to school busing
c.   the exclusion of blacks and other minorities from private clubs
d.   the high unemployment rate among black teenagers

16. The sociologist William Julius Wilson has argued that:
    a. blacks and whites have equal opportunities in America today
    b. opportunities for black Americans have not changed in the last quarter-century
    c. racial inequality persists because of continuing prejudice and discrimination
    d. racial inequality persists because of lingering social-class differences

17. Which of the following is an example of affirmative action?
    a. the federal prohibition on granting government contracts to firms that discriminate against minorities
    b. the 1963 March on Washington
    c. a plan to recruit minority members for a police force
    d. laws against discrimination in education, employment, and housing

18. In recent years, the education gap between blacks and whites has:
    a. remained about the same
    b. narrowed
    c. widened somewhat
    d. widened substantially

19. The Latino population includes three main ethnic groups. Which of the following is NOT one of these?
    a. Portuguese Americans
    b. Mexican Americans
    c. Puerto Ricans
    d. Cuban Americans

20. Which of the following groups has the lowest life expectancy of any racial or ethnic group in American society?
    a. Mexican Americans
    b. Aleuts
    c. American Indians
    d. Eskimos

Answers

1. b: In terms of racial categories, what matters is that people *believe* that there are innate, genetic differences among categories of human beings and that these differences are *meaningful*. (Races and Ethnic Groups; p. 316)

2. a: Ethnic groups are maintained by "consciousness of kind" and the assumption that people who share your ethnic background are likely to have similar values. (Races and Ethnic Groups; p. 316)

3. b: The poor are disadvantaged, held in low esteem, and involuntarily confined to their status, but they do not have the group consciousness or feeling of solidarity that Louis Wirth saw as a defining characteristic of minority groups. (Minority Groups; p. 317)

4. c: Wirth specified four key points: disadvantage, low esteem, involuntary membership, and self-consciousness of being a "people apart." (Minority Groups; p. 317)

5. d: The existence of minority groups implies the existence of a majority group, which is able to impose its norms and values on others (Minority Groups; p. 319).

6. a: There was a good deal of cultural exchange and intermarriage in colonial Brazil, leading to amalgamation. (Patterns of Intergroup Relations; p. 321)

7. c: People may accept and even enjoy ethnic and racial diversity in their public lives, yet resist close connections. (Patterns of Intergroup Relations; p. 321)

8. d: All over the U.S., ethnic and racial groups can be observed maintaining their own language, religion, and customs, and socializing mainly among themselves, thus maintaining their distinct identity, but participating jointly with the members of other racial and ethnic groups in the same political and economic systems. (Patterns of Intergroup Relations; p. 321)

9. a: In the United States today, there is much debate about whether our institutions should promote assimilation or harmonious pluralism; multiculturalists advocate cultural diversity. (Patterns of Intergroup Relations; p. 322)

10. c: The four patterns of intergroup relations are: amalgamation, assimilation, pluralism, and exploitation. (Patterns of Intergroup

Relations; pp. 321-323)

11.   b: Apartheid is a philosophy of white supremacy and a system designed to maintain the separation of the races. (A Global View: South Africa and The Legacy of Apartheid; p. 324)

12.   b: The Southwest was won by force of arms. In theory, Hispanics were guaranteed full rights as citizens under the Treaty of Guadalupe Hidalgo (1848); in practice, most were overwhelmed by Anglo settlers and Anglo courts of justice. (Racial and Ethnic Relations in the United States: Changing Patterns; pp. 329-330)

13.   d: Criticisms of Herrnstein and Murray's work included *all* of these issues. (Innate Differences: Real or Imagined?; pp. 334-335)

14.   b: Prejudice rests on stereotypes: over generalizations about a group and its members that go beyond existing evidence. (Prejudice and Discrimination; p. 336)

15.   d: Undoubtedly, some employers turn down teenaged applicants simply because they are black; these are acts of individual racism. But the high unemployment *rate* among black teenagers is an unintended consequence. (Institutionalized Racism; p. 339)

16.   d: William Julius Wilson believes that there is substantial social inequality between blacks and whites; that opportunities for black Americans have changed in the last twenty-five years; but that racial inequality persists not so much because of lingering prejudice and discrimination, but rather because of lingering social-class differences. (Race or Class?; pp. 339-340)

17.   c: Affirmative action programs are controversial because they are not color blind, but require some degree of *reverse discrimination* to ensure that minorities are not excluded. (Minority Rights and Affirmative Action; pp. 342-343)

18.   b: In terms of the median years of school completed, blacks and whites are almost equal, but equal quantity of education does not necessarily mean equal quality. (Racial and Ethnic Inequality in the United States Today: African Americans; p. 344)

19.   a: The three categories are: Mexican Americans, Puerto Ricans, and Cuban Americans. (Racial and Ethnic Inequality in the United States Today: Latinos; p. 348)

20.   c: American Indians are one of the most disadvantaged groups in our society; their life expectancy is ten years shorter than the average. (Racial and Ethnic Inequality in the United States

Today: Native Americans; p. 350)

CRITICAL THINKING

1. Minority groups are not necessarily smaller than other groups; rather, their members are regarded as inferior in some way by dominant groups. Have you ever been discriminated against because of your race, sex, age, or some other characteristic? What did the discrimination involve? Did you feel that you or the group you belong to was being exploited by another group? Can you locate the source of this discrimination in competition or some other element of the social structure?

2. Government legislation such as affirmative action and programs such as school busing are designed to help minority groups of all kinds, yet each such effort has its staunch critics for one reason or another. Overall, do you think that these programs are helping or hurting race and ethnic relations in the United States?

WEB EXERCISE: Evaluating Herrnstein and Murray's *The Bell Curve* on the Internet

The text's discussion of Herrnstein and Murray's *The Bell Curve* provides a general impression of how much controversy has been generated as a result of this publication.

This controversy is well represented on the Internet. Here are a few sites that you may wish to visit in order to learn more about these controversial issues:

http://search.princeton.edu/index/ (Then, search for "bell curve")

http://www.apa.org/journals/bell.html

http://usatoday.com./life/health/lhs064.htm

http://www.siam.org/siamnews/bookrevs/case195.htm

If you encounter difficulty in accessing these sites, use one of the Search

Engines on the Internet (Excite, Lycos, Yahoo, AltaVista, etc.) to locate other descriptive sites, using the key words: Bell Curve.

Chapter Ten

GENDER STRATIFICATION

OBJECTIVES

After reading Chapter Ten, you should be able to provide detailed responses to the following questions:

1. What is gender?
2. How different are the sexes?
3. What are the social and economic consequences of being female in American society?
4. What are the sociological explanations of gender stratification?
5. What are the origins of the women's movement and what is its future?
6. How are men and our perceptions of masculinity changing?
7. Are attitudes toward sexual orientation changing?

CHAPTER REVIEW

I. What is gender?

Sex refers to the biological differences between males and females; *sex role* refers to the behaviors, attitudes, and motivations that a particular culture considers appropriate for males or females; and *gender* refers to the complex of social meanings that is attached to biological sex. Gender is a social institution; it involves differences in power; and it is a cultural construct.

II. How different are the sexes?

Males and females play different roles in reproduction, but other differences, like brain hemispheres, thinking, and athletic performances, have been exaggerated. The problem with biological theories of gender differences is that they draw attention away from gender stratification.

Gender stratification is universal, but the roles men and women play in different cultures vary and there are differing degrees of inequality. Cross-cultural studies show that ideas about what is appropriate masculine and feminine behavior also vary widely. Whatever the ideas, parents and others go to great lengths to distinguish girls from boys and to socialize them appropriately. There are pervasive differences in sex role socialization and, given their magnitude, it is surprising that sex differences are not greater than they are. Although these differences in socialization are vast, the surprise is that boys and girls are more alike than different; most researchers conclude that there are no significant distinctions between the sexes in cognitive style, creativity, independence, susceptibility to influence, general self-esteem, and so forth.

Even though males and females are more alike than different, in virtually every realm, men are considered the norm and women are seen as "abnormal." This is what Tavris calls the "mismeasure of women"; she maintains that we tend to assume that "equal" means "the same." For Tavris, until we develop *human* standards, and recognize the fact that women can be different and equal, gender bias and discrimination are likely to persist.

III.   Why are women, who represent 52 percent of the population, a minority group in the United States?

Although they represent a numerical majority, women in America fit Wirth's definition of a minority group; they are not treated as equals and are aware of discrimination (the objective and subjective criteria for a minority group).

In the workplace, women earn less than men with comparable education and experience; they tend to be segregated in low-income, low-prestige service occupations; the pay gap narrowed in the 1980s, but women are still far behind men. To a high degree, the job market is still segregated by gender. *Comparable worth* is the effort to correct gender bias in wages. But even female executives find that they are trapped under a *glass ceiling*, which translates into lost dollars and cents. In addition, women encounter hidden cultural and structural obstacles to getting ahead, including prejudice against working mothers and sexual harassment. The press dubbed the lower tier for female workers the "mommy track." And, women encounter another problem that rarely touches men: *sexual harassment*.

In the family, women still bear the primary responsibility for housework and child care, whether they work or not, and "pay" more for divorce than men do.

In a classic study, Arlie Hochschild and her colleagues coined the phrase "the second shift," referring to the phenomenon of women who work outside of their homes on a full-time basis, but are still responsible for nearly all housework responsibilities.

Contemporary, "no-fault" divorce laws were written with the intention of treating both parties fairly, but such legislation has caused many women more harm than good.

IV.   What are the sociological explanations of gender stratification?

Sociologists differ in their views of the causes of gender stratification. The two main sociological perspectives differ both on whether the gender gap exists and what should be done about it. *Functionalists* see gender stratification as the product of a biologically based division of labor that, up until recently, benefitted both sexes. In contrast, *conflict theorists* see gender stratification as a design to maintain male privilege and appease working men.

In explaining specific areas of gender stratification, sociologists often employ *middle-range* theories, including human capital theory, overcrowding theory, and the dual labor market hypothesis. Underlying all these middle-range theories is the belief that prejudice and discrimination, based on stereotypes of sex differences in abilities, keep women "in their place." The explanation of persistent gender inequality lies in *institutionalized sexism*: established social patterns that have the unintended consequence of limiting women's opportunities.

V.   What are the origins of the women's movement and what is its future?

Feminism is not a modern phenomenon. The early women's movement emerged during a period of rapid social change in the late nineteenth century. Feminism seemed to disappear in the early twentieth century, after women won the vote, but resurfaced in the 1960s--another period of "social" upheaval. A number of factors contributed to the resurgence of feminism in the 1960s and 1970s: a climate of social change launched by the civil rights movement and culminating in the antiwar movement; the emergence of a sense of collective injustice; organization; and structural change. After a period of more or less steady victories in the 1970s, the movement encountered organized, government-backed opposition in the 1980s. But setbacks seem to have strengthened women's resolve to press for support of their family roles, as well as equality in the workplace. The women's movement has become institutionalized.

VI.   How are men and our perceptions of masculinity changing?

Often overlooked is the fact that gender stratification affects males as well as females, most obviously in terms of their health: Males are more vulnerable than females to various health problems at every age.

Old cultural definitions of what it means to be a man, especially the "good provider" role, remain powerful: In our society, a man's status depends on what he does for a living and how successful he is in his occupation. Despite this, new ideas are emerging, such as the image of the "new father." Our culture's definition of what it means to be a "good" father is changing. Masculinity is being redefined.

VII.   Are attitudes toward sexual orientation changing?

Much as our social institutions are based on the assumption that men and women are inherently different, so they assume that the only "normal" or "natural" form of sexual interaction is between adults of the opposite sex. Being gay or lesbian constitutes a social identity that shapes the way other members of society view a person and how they interact with him or her. Attitudes toward homosexual behavior have varied with the time and place. Not all traditional societies approve or tolerate homosexuality. In general, Judeo-Christian teachings have condemned homosexuality. The medicalization of homosexuality did not lead to greater tolerance, but the reverse. *Homophobia* became entrenched. Social attitudes toward homosexuality have changed, but prejudice and hate crimes against gays and lesbians have not disappeared.

CONCEPT REVIEW

Match each of the following terms with the correct definition.

a. gender (p. 361)
b. comparable worth (p. 369)
c. institutionalized sexism
    (p. 385)
d. sex role (p. 361)
e. feminism (p. 385)

f. sex (p. 361)
g. sexual orientation (p. 361)
h. glass ceiling (p. 370)
i. homophobia (p. 395)
j. sexual harassment (p. 372)

1.___ Established social patterns that have the unintended consequence of limiting women's opportunities.
2.___ The complex of social meanings that is attached to biological sex.
3.___ The behavior, attitudes, and motivations that a particular culture considers appropriate for males or females.
4.___ An individual's attraction to the members of the opposite, same, or both sexes.
5.___ The belief that women are equal to men and should have equal rights and opportunities.
6.___ A person's biological identity as male or female.
7.___ The effort to correct gender bias in wages.
8.___ Subtle, even invisible, barriers to the advancement of female executives.
9.___ Refers to behavior wherein an employee is forced by an employer to be sexually intimate, or to a "hostile working environment."
10.___ Prejudice and discrimination against gay people; the equivalent of sexism and racism.

Answers

1.	c	5.	e	9.	j
2.	a	6.	f	10.	i
3.	d	7.	b		
4.	g	8.	h		

REVIEW QUESTIONS

1.   The term *sex role* refers to:
    a.   a person's biological identity as male or female
    b.   the behavior and attitudes people consider appropriate for males and females
    c.   an individual's inner sense of being masculine or feminine
    d.   biological differences at birth

2.   The problem with biological theories of gender differences is that they:
    a.   draw attention away from gender similarities
    b.   draw attention to gender similarities
    c.   ignore basic differences between males and females
    d.   none of the above

3.   Studies on gender socialization indicate that contemporary parents:
    a.   perceive male and female babies as similar
    b.   treat male and female babies the same
    c.   engage in more talk with male babies
    d.   feel that male and female babies behave differently

4.   According to Carol Tavris, in virtually every realm, men are considered the norm and women are seen as "abnormal," deficient--the sex that needs to be explained. Tavris refers to this situation as the:
    a.   abnormal female
    b.   universal male
    c.   male hero syndrome
    d.   female weirdos

5.   The text points out that female physicians tend to be:
    a.   neurosurgeons
    b.   thoracic surgeons
    c.   pediatricians
    d.   orthopedic surgeons

6.   Suppose that an employer conducts a job-evaluation of male- and female-dominated occupations and assigns each a numerical score for degrees of difficulty; ideally, the pay for female jobs would then be raised to the level of male jobs with the same or similar scores. This procedure exemplifies:
a.   job accounting
b.   gender destratification
c.   anti-sex discrimination
d.   comparable worth

7.   The text points out that very few women make it to the top of corporate ladders or government bureaucracies; less than 5 percent of senior managers (at or above the level of vice president) in the Fortune 500 and Service 500 corporations are women; rather, they work in middle management. This situation is referred to as the:
a.   glass ceiling
b.   sticky floor
c.   velvet hammer
d.   pink wall

8.   Arlie Hochschild spent three summers observing and interviewing managers and employees at a Fortune 500 company with a reputation for "family friendly" policies. To her surprise, she found that parents did not take advantage of offers of flexible jobs and schedules. Consciously or unconsciously, women feared being shunted onto a _____ of lower-level jobs, interrupted careers, and part-time work.
a.   pink-collar trap
b.   last sexual barrier
c.   mommy track
d.   harassment tier

9.   Suppose that the women who work for Joe's Construction Company are exposed to unwanted and denigrating sexual jokes, erotic pinups, remarks about their appearance, and groping. These female workers are the victims of:
     a.   stereotyping
     b.   sexual harassment
     c.   nothing unusual
     d.   poor sportsmanship

10. Which of the following is NOT one of Arlie Hochschild's three basic orientations toward sex roles?
     a.   traditional
     b.   transitional
     c.   egalitarian
     d.   authoritarian

11. The text points out that in many ways, the world's girls and women are:
     a.   "missing persons"
     b.   "covert prostitutes"
     c.   victims of gesellschaft
     d.   none of the above

12. Functionalists maintain that gender stratification is rooted in:
     a.   the exploitation of the weak by the strong
     b.   the biological differences between the sexes
     c.   selective perception and social definition
     d.   power and authority

13. Conflict theorists see gender inequality as:
     a.   a function of the biological differences between the sexes
     b.   a matter of social definition
     c.   part of the universal problem of exploitation of the weak by the strong
     d.   beneficial for society

14. Which of the following is NOT one of the middle-range theories of gender stratification discussed in the text?
   a. major market theory
   b. human capital theory
   c. overcrowding theory
   d. dual labor market

15. In which of the following ways is the contemporary women's movement like the early feminist movement?
   a. Both had grass-roots support.
   b. Both developed in climates of social change and were to some extent by-products of other social movements.
   c. Both practiced single-issue politics.
   d. Both were short-lived.

16. Which of the following is NOT one of the factors mentioned in the text that contributed to the resurgence of feminism in the 1960s and 1970s?
   a. a climate of social change launched by the civil rights movement and culminating in the antiwar movement
   b. the emergence of a sense of collective injustice
   c. structural change
   d. disorganization

17. Which of the following is *false*?
   a. More males than females are miscarried, stillborn, or die in their first year of life.
   b. American men are more likely than women to die from heart disease, lung disease, and cirrhosis of the liver.
   c. Men attempt suicide more often than women.
   d. Men are almost four times as likely to be victims of homicide.

18. The association of masculinity with the provider role:
   a. dates to the Bible
   b. is part of ancient history
   c. is relatively recent
   d. none of the above

19. According to the text's discussion of sexual orientation:
   a. our culture defines homosexuality on a continuum rather than as an either/or characteristic
   b. gay and lesbian reflect a social identity that shapes the way other members of society view a person and how they interact with him or her
   c. attitudes toward homosexual behavior have remained the same with the time and place
   d. most traditional societies have approved and tolerated homosexuality

20. The medicalization of homosexuality did not lead to greater tolerance, but the reverse: Prejudice and discrimination against gays, the equivalent of sexism and racism, became entrenched, which is referred to as
   a. homophobia
   b. homosexism
   c. homosegregation
   d. homomania

Answers

1. b: Sociologists distinguish between cultural definitions of masculinity and femininity (sex roles), the biological differences between males and females (sex), and the complex of social meanings that is attached to biological sex (gender). (Defining Gender; p. 361)

2. a: Studies reporting that the sexes are more alike than different rarely make news. (Biological Differences; p. 363)

3. d: Parents today say that they have the same socialization goals for males and females (they want both to be neat, both to be athletic, and so on). But they also say that their male and female children behave differently. (Gender Socialization; pp. 365-366)

4. b: The "universal male" is so ingrained in our thinking that we often fail to notice him. ("The Mismeasure of Women"; p. 366)

5. c: When women do go into prestigious and high-paying fields, it is usually into positions that are lower in pay, authority, and status than men's jobs in the same field; moreover, women who have entered professions often specialize within those professions.

(Gender Segregation; p. 369)

6.   d: Comparable worth is the effort to correct gender bias in wages; the idea is that male and female jobs that require the comparable skill, training, effort, responsibility, and ability to cope with unpleasant conditions should pay the same. (Gender Segregation; p. 369)

7.   a: The typical female executive earns only two-thirds of what male executives earn; and she is the exception to the rule, due to the glass ceiling. (Job Mobility; p. 370)

8.   c: Schwartz was misquoted as advising that companies institutionalize the inequalities that exist now between mothers and nonmothers. (Work and Family; pp. 371-372)

9.   b: Recent examples of sexual harassment in the news are the Clarence Thomas, Tailhook, and Paula Jones incidents. (Work and Sex; p. 372)

10.   d: Hochschild's typology was constructed through her research involving intensive interviews with fifty dual-earner families over a six-year period and observation of a dozen families in their homes. ("The Second Shift"; p. 376)

11.   a: Statistics show that girls and women are "missing" from schools, from the paid labor force, from the halls of power and decision making, and from the battlefield. (A Global View: Women as "Missing Persons"; pp. 380-381)

12.   b: Functionalists argue that expectations have to be brought back in line with actual conditions; some advocate a return to traditional roles and the stable families those roles produced; others urge a redefinition of gender roles, to allow both sexes to participate equally in public (work-oriented) and private (family-oriented) life. (Sociological Perspectives on Gender Stratification; p. 379)

13.   c: According to the conflict view, men used their superior strength and women's vulnerability to create institutions that supported and maintained male power and authority; men controlled the means of production, and women were seen as men's domestic servants. (Conflict Theory; pp. 379; 384)

14.   a: Underlying all of the middle-range theories discussed is the belief that prejudice and discrimination, based on stereotypes of sex differences in abilities, keep women "in their place." (Middle-Range Theories of Gender Stratification; pp. 384-385)

15.   b: Many of the early suffrage activists were females who had been turned away by the abolitionist and other movements; many of the founders of the contemporary women's movement were activists in the civil rights and anti-Vietnam war movements who found that male activists considered female concerns trivial. (Equality For Women: A Century of Struggle; pp. 385-387)

16.   d: The women's movement did not create the desire to be "more than a housewife" or propel women into the labor force; rather, the movement was a reflection of a general climate of social change, or rising expectations among female activists and the fact that many women were already working and pursuing higher education. (The Modern Women's Movement; pp. 386-387)

17.   c: Women attempt suicide more often than men, but men succeed in killing themselves three times as often. (The Hazards of Being Male; pp. 389-390)

18.   c: Throughout much of human history, women played a vital role in providing for their families. The concept of the provider as a specialized male role dates to the Industrial Revolution and the emergence of a wage economy. (The "Good Provider"; p. 390)

19.   b: Our culture defines homosexuality as an either/or characteristic; attitudes toward homosexual behavior have varied with the time and place; and not all traditional societies approve or tolerate homosexuality. (Sexual Orientation; pp. 395-396)

20.   a: Homophobia refers to prejudice and discrimination against gay people, and is the equivalent of sexism and racism; the other choices are nonsensical. (Sexual Orientation; pp. 395-396)

CRITICAL THINKING

1.   In this chapter, a number of forms of discrimination that are experienced by women and men are discussed. Can you locate other types of discrimination--either explicit or subtle--that are not mentioned in the text. Have you experienced any types of discrimination yourself? What should be done to rectify these problems?

2.   Use the principle of comparable worth to evaluate different employment categories at your college or university. Are there some jobs, held mostly

by men, that involve the same training and responsibility but pay higher than other jobs that are held mostly by women? Should this situation be rectified? If so, how?

WEB EXERCISE: Women in the Military

There is ongoing controversy about women's roles in the military, especially in reference to their participation in combat. There are a number of dedicated sites on the Internet that deal with women in the military and offer the visitor an opportunity to evaluate the many issues involved:

http://www.militarywoman.org/

http://userpages.aug.com/captbarb/

http://www.gendergap.com/ (click on "women in the military")

PART FOUR

SOCIAL INSTITUTIONS

Chapter Eleven

THE FAMILY

OBJECTIVES

After reading Chapter Eleven, you should be able to provide detailed answers to the following questions:

1. How do families vary across cultures?
2. How have American families changed?
3. How do today's Americans choose a marriage partner, decide to marry, and balance work and family roles?
4. How do sociologists explain family violence?
5. What are the causes and consequences of today's high divorce rate?
6. What is the future of the American family and what will it look like?

CHAPTER REVIEW

I. **How do families vary across cultures?**

All known societies have families, but the structure and function of this social institution vary considerably. *Polygamy* (marriage involving more than one wife or husband at the same time) is the preferred form of marriage in 75 percent of human societies; most often, this pattern takes the form of *polygyny*, or marriage of one man to two or more women. In contrast, only four societies have been reported in which *polyandry* (marriage of one woman to two or more men) is the norm. *Monogamy* involves marriage between only one woman and one man, and this pattern is the preferred form of marriage in only 25 percent of the world's societies. *Group marriage* refers to marriage of two or more men to two or more women at the same time, and is the rarest family type; some have debated whether this pattern exists at all. Some Americans practice *serial monogamy*: one exclusive, legally sanctioned, but relatively short-lived marriage after another.

In most traditional societies, the family is the basic unit of social structure and performs four key functions: the regulation of sex; the replacement of members (reproduction); the socialization of children; and the distribution of goods and services (or economics). In modern societies, other institutions have taken over all or part of these functions. But the family has taken on a new function: emotional gratification.

II.   How have American families changed?

Families not only vary from culture to culture, but they change over time within a single social organization. In our society during the 1950s, the multigenerational extended family gave way to the ideal of independent nuclear families, but the text notes that extended families were not as common, nor were nuclear families as isolated as many people imagine; hence the term *modified extended family*. Family ties remain strong, however. A majority of Americans keep in touch with their extended families, looking to them for financial aid and help with daily problems.

The major change in the American family in recent decades involves *variety*. Today, most Americans live in a variety of family types over the course of their lifetimes: Singlehood, single parenthood, and childless marriages have all increased dramatically in the past two or three decades. For most individuals, however, these are temporary arrangements before, between, and/or after conventional marriage. In fact, in recent years, extended or multigeneration households are making a comeback. These households constitute the *new extended family*.

Ethnic and racial variations add to the diversity of family life in America. African-American families typically have strong extended family ties; Latino families are distinguished by their strong sense of familism; while Asian-American families are strictly patriarchal.

III. How do contemporary Americans choose a mate, decide to get married, and balance work with family roles?

Despite changes in the family, the great majority of Americans get married and become parents. Although women today wait somewhat longer to get married than they did in the past, over 95 percent of Americans marry at least once in their lives; indeed, the U.S. has one of the highest marriage rates in the world.

Most Americans assume that people get married because they are in love (or, at least this is the way things should be, according to most members of our society). But, love is not random. Most people marry someone who is like themselves in terms of religion, education, and other attributes that society considers important: these are the rules of *homogamy*. Exchange theory portrays courtship as an exchange of assets and liabilities in which people weigh the costs and benefits of a potential partner. Most women marry a man who is a few years older than they are. The most important criteria in mate selection are economic security and family background, not mutual attraction.

Unmarried couples living together have become more common and more socially acceptable in recent years, but most couples see living together as a stage in courtship, not as a substitute for marriage.

One of the major issues confronting married couples in the 1990s has been how to combine work and family life. A majority of married women are employed today, but working women are not a modern phenomenon. Regardless of whether or not they have a full-time job, and no matter how much they earn, wives devote significantly more time to housework than husbands do; almost 80 percent of all household chores are performed by women. In 1995, 21 million American children under age 6 had mothers who were employed outside their homes. With wives working, the daily routine may become more hectic, but there is little evidence that two careers either harm or improve the quality of family life.

IV. How do sociologists explain family violence?

All families do not live happily ever after. Recent surveys have shown that violence in the family is more common than most people imagine at all socioeconomic levels. There are other myths about family violence. In fact, only about 10 percent of abusers are diagnosed as mentally ill; abuse occurs in a variety of social classes; alcohol and drugs are not the real causes of family violence; all abused children do not necessarily become abusing parents; and battered wives do not enjoy being hurt.

The potential for violence is built into the family; many of the characteristics we cherish most about families (e.g., *intimacy* and *privacy*) also make us most vulnerable. Another factor is *inequality*. Furthermore, and perhaps most disturbing, there is a good deal of *social and cultural support* for the use of physical force in the family. And, in the process of *socialization*, we learn to associate violence with the family.

Three decades of research have shown that virtually any family or intimate relationship has the potential to become violent. Infants and very young children are at greatest risk of abuse and most likely to be severely injured or even die as a result. Violence between adults who are attached to one another begins before couples become committed and continues or sometimes escalates if they separate. Male victimization has been the subject of much controversy. Family violence is not limited to spouses and lovers or to parents who abuse their children. Children also abuse their parents. In short, no one is immune to violence by the people they love (or are supposed to love).

V.   What are the causes and consequences of today's high divorce rate?

The divorce rate reached an all-time high in the United States in 1979, and the number of divorces involving children has grown. At current rates, at least half of marriages formed today are likely to end in divorce, but all marriages do not have an equal chance of success or failure; some segments of our population are more prone to divorce than others. The likelihood of divorce is correlated with age at first marriage (younger marrieds are more prone to divorce); socioeconomic status (divorce rates are highest in lower socioeconomic groups); race (most studies report that black couples are more likely to divorce than white couples); religion (divorce rates are higher for Protestants than Catholics, although separation rates are higher for Catholics); and children (birth of a first child reduces the chances of divorce, but subsequent births have little effect).

Among the factors contributing to the high divorce rate are: changes in the divorce laws making it easier and faster to end a marriage; the movement of women into the labor force; a general shift from faith in institutions to concern with individual fulfillment; and the fact that formal marriage may have lost some of its cultural significance.

Each year, about 1 million children -- almost 2 percent of all children in the United States -- are involved in a divorce, but this is only a fraction of the number of children who have been or will be directly affected. Recent research suggests that divorce has debilitating effects on children, but that some children are not as adversely affected as others, and most children recover in a year or two.

The high rate of remarriage after divorce and the number of *blended families* indicate that people believe as strongly in the institution of marriage as they ever did.

VI.   What is the future of the American family, and what will it look like?

Some social scientists are pessimistic about the family's future. David Popenoe maintains that the American family is becoming weaker; that the disintegration of the family is behind many of our most urgent social problems; and that the heart of the problem lies in the steady break-up of the two-parent home.

Other observers are cautiously optimistic, maintaining that the idea that contemporary American families are in crisis is based on a misreading of history; that to blame society's ills on families is to "blame the victim"; and that whether one is optimistic or pessimistic depends in part on how one defines the family.

Still, even the optimists are concerned, especially about the future of our children. One family sociologist, Arlene Skolnick, has referred to the family as an "embattled paradise," which captures the ambivalence most people feel toward the family.

CONCEPT REVIEW

Match each of the following terms with the correct definition.

a.   divorce rate (p. 431)
b.   homogamy (p. 419)
c.   monogamy (p. 405)
d.   polyandry (p. 405)
e.   polygyny (p. 405)
f.   new extended family (p. 417)
g.   serial monogamy (p. 406)
h.   blended family (p. 435)
i.   polygamy (p. 405)
j.   nuclear family (p. 408)
k.   modified extended family (p. 408)
l.   extended family (p. 408)
m.   group marriage (p. 405)
n.   family (p. 405)

1.___   A marriage involving only one woman and one man.
2.___   The number of divorces per 1,000 married women (or men) age 15 or older in a given year.
3.___   A network of relatives who live in separate residences, often miles apart, but maintain ties with each other.
4.___   The term used to describe households made up of single adults or single parents living with their parents or other relatives.
5.___   A husband, his wife, and their dependent children living in a home of their own.
6.___   The marriage of one man to two or more women at the same time.
7.___   One exclusive, legally sanctioned, but relatively short-lived marriage after another.
8.___   The tendency to marry someone who is like ourselves in the social attributes our society considers important.
9.___   Members of three or more generations, related by blood or marriage, who live together or in close proximity.
10.___   The marriage of one woman to two or more men at the same time.
11.___   Family situations that include combinations of at least one spouse with children from a previous marriage.
12.___   Marriage involving more than one wife or husband at the same time.
13.___   Marriage of two or more men to two or more women at the same time.
14.___   A social group, and social institution, with an identifiable structure based on positions and interaction among people who occupy those positions.

Answers

1.	c	6.	e	11.	h
2.	a	7.	g	12.	i
3.	k	8.	b	13.	m
4.	f	9.	l	14.	n
5.	j	10.	d		

REVIEW QUESTIONS

1.   The most *preferred* form of marriage in human societies is:
      a.   monogamy
      b.   polygamy
      c.   bigamy
      d.   polyandry

2.   According to the text, _____ is the rarest family type, with some debate about whether this arrangement exists at all.
      a.   polygyny
      b.   polyandry
      c.   group marriage
      d.   bigamy

3.   The function of family that has become increasingly important in contemporary society is:
      a.   the distribution of goods and services
      b.   socialization of children
      c.   regulation of sexual activity
      d.   emotional gratification

4.   Which western nation has the highest rate of teenage pregnancy?
      a.   the United States
      b.   Canada
      c.   France
      d.   England

5.   In the early 1990s, less than half of adults under age 35 were the head (or married to the head) of an independent family household. These households constitute the _____ family.
      a.   modified extended
      b.   modified nuclear
      c.   new extended
      d.   bilateral

6.   Which of the following is NOT a characteristic of African-American families?
    a.   They tend to be middle-aged.
    b.   They often live in cities or in southern states.
    c.   They are more likely than other families to be headed by a woman.
    d.   Almost half of these families include two parents.

7.   Which of the following is NOT a characteristic of Latino families?
    a.   They tend to be young.
    b.   They are characterized by a strong sense of individualism.
    c.   They experience high levels of poverty.
    d.   They display high birth rates.

8.   Which of the following is NOT a characteristic of Asian-American families?
    a.   Even when Asian-American women work, as many do, they assume nearly total responsibility for housework and child rearing.
    b.   Marriage rates are very high and divorce rates lower than average.
    c.   Children defer to their parents' wishes.
    d.   They tend to be strictly matriarchal.

9.   Which of the following illustrates the principle of *homogamy*?
    a.   marrying someone who lives within walking distance
    b.   marrying someone with similar marital experience (never married, divorced, or widowed)
    c.   opposites attract
    d.   marrying for love

10.   Which of the following is NOT characteristic of cohabitation?
    a.   Living together is a step toward marriage.
    b.   Couples who live together before marriage have higher divorce rates than other couples.
    c.   For most couples, cohabitation is a substitute for marriage.
    d.   None of the above

11. Almost _____ percent of all household chores are performed by women.
   a. 30
   b. 55
   c. 80
   d. 100

12. How much time a father devotes to child care depends on:
   a. the wife's schedule
   b. the number of hours the mother works
   c. whether or not the mother believes the father is competent at child care
   d. all of the above

13. According to the text's discussion of the impact of work on families:
   a. employed wives tend to be unhappy in comparison to full-time homemakers
   b. marital satisfaction tends to be highest among working wives with lower levels of education
   c. married women are most likely to be depressed when they are working, and would rather be at home full time
   d. the less time working couples spend together, the less likely they are to be satisfied with their marriage

14. Which of the following is NOT a myth concerning family violence?
   a. Family violence is rare.
   b. Abuse occurs only in poor, minority families.
   c. Children who are victims of family violence are more likely to be abusive as adults than are children who did not experience family violence.
   d. Abusers are mentally ill.

15.   The text points out that the potential for violence is built into the family and that many of the characteristics we cherish most about families also make people vulnerable within them. Which of the following is NOT one of these characteristics?
  a.   intimacy
  b.   privacy
  c.   social and cultural support
  d.   equality

16.   According to the text's discussion of intimate violence:
  a.   women are at the greatest risk of abuse and most likely to be severely injured or die as a result
  b.   violence between adults usually does not occur before they become committed
  c.   children do not abuse their parents
  d.   none of the above

17.   According to the text's discussion of male victimization:
  a.   early studies found that female violence toward men they love (or had loved) was almost as common as the reverse
  b.   women usually engage in a pattern of violent abuse
  c.   anecdotal evidence and case studies suggest that men and women are equally likely to stalk and kill their victims
  d.   all of the above

18.   Which of the following is/are important factors in terms of who gets divorced?
  a.   age at first marriage
  b.   socioeconomic status
  c.   race
  d.   all of the above

19.   Estimates are that _____ of all children will participate in a blended family before they reach age 18.
  a.   one-fourth
  b.   one-third
  c.   one-half
  d.   three-quarters

20.   Family sociologist Arlene Skolnick has referred to today's family as a/an:
a.   embattled paradise
b.   fractured institution
c.   shattered social system
d.   none of the above

Answers

1.   b: In 75 percent of human societies, the preferred arrangement is polygamy; monogamy is preferred in only 25 percent of the world's societies; polyandry has been reported in only four societies. (Family Structure; p. 405)

2.   c: Group marriage is most likely in a society where polyandry is the cultural ideal, but if the first wife proves infertile, a second wife joins the marriage to provide children. (Family Structure; p. 405)

3.   d: Although schools teach children skills, the family still provides emotional support and caring; the modern family is an "intimate environment." (Family Functions; p. 407)

4.   a: Each year, more than a million American teenagers become pregnant, even though teenagers in Canada and Europe have as high or higher rates of sexual activity. (Single Parent Families; p. 416)

5.   c: In recent years, extended or multigeneration households are making a comeback as single adults return to their parents' household. (The New Extended Family; p. 417)

6.   a: African-American families tend to be *young*; contrary to popular stereotypes, 48 percent of these families include two parents. (African-American Families; p. 418)

7.   b: In comparison to other groups, Latino families are distinguished by their strong sense of familism: *la familia*. (Latino Families; p. 418)

8.   d: Asian-American families are strictly patriarchal; men are the wage earners, decision makers, and disciplinarians. (Asian-American Families; p. 418)

9.   b: Conforming to the principle of homogamy, a majority of Americans have chosen to marry people of their own race, religion, social class, and (approximate) age. With so many

divorces and remarriages, marital status has been added to this list. (Courtship, Marriage, and Children; p. 419)

10.   c: Only a very small percentage of couples see cohabitation as a substitute for marriage; for most, it is a stage similar to engagement. (Living Together; pp. 421-422)

11.   c: Regardless of whether they have a full-time job or not and no matter how much they earn, wives devote significantly more time to housework than husbands do. (Housework; p. 422)

12.   d: All of these are factors affecting the amount of time fathers devote to child care. In addition, the father's relationship with his own father is important. And, if the child is a boy, the father is more likely to be involved. (Child Care; p. 423)

13.   d: Time together is a problem for most working couples. The less time they spend together, the less likely they are to be satisfied with their marriage. Employed wives tend to be quite happy in comparison with full-time homemakers. Marital satisfaction tends to be highest among working wives with higher levels of education. Married women are quite satisfied with working outside of the home.(The Impact of Work on Families; pp. 423-425)

14.   c: Although this statement is true, it is a myth that all children who are abused grow up to be abusers; not all abused children become abusive parents. (Behind Closed Doors: Violence in the Family; pp. 425-427)

15.   d: From a feminist perspective, violence toward women is a function of inequality and an extension of male dominance in society as a whole. (Behind Closed Doors: Violence in the Family/Sociological Explanations; pp. 427-428)

16.   d: Infants and very young children are at greatest risk of abuse and most likely to be severely injured or even die as a result; violence between adults who are attached to one another begins before couples become committed; and children also abuse their parents. (Intimate Violence: The Victims; pp. 428-430)

17.   a: Although early studies found that female violence toward men they love (or had loved) was almost as common as the reverse, closer analysis found that female violence often occurs as self-defense and that women inflict less injury than men do; anecdotal evidence and case studies suggest that men are more likely to stalk

and kill their victims. (Intimate Adults; pp. 429-430)

18.   d: Socioeconomic status, age at first marriage, and race all help determine the likelihood of divorce. (Who Gets Divorced and Why; pp. 431-432)

19.   b: About eight in ten remarriages involve children, and as a result, more than 7 million children live with a stepparent today. (Remarriage and Blended Families; p. 435)

20.   a: Skolnick's terminology is a seeming contradiction in terms, but the phrase captures the ambivalence that most people feel toward family. (The Future of the Family; p. 438)

CRITICAL THINKING

1.   In American society, the normative arrangement for marriage and the family is monogamy. Suppose that the prevailing norms changed to permit polygyny or polyandry--how might this affect social relationships? If it were a sign of social prestige for a woman to have several husbands, for example, how might the power relationships between men and women change?

2.   Some observers of the family in American society have commented that as an institution, the family is "searching for a future." Others insist that the future is already here and that the family has a bright tomorrow. In the light of the text's discussion, consider what the future of the family may be like. What are the plans of your friends and acquaintances about marriage and family issues? Do they plan to marry? What other alternatives do they consider?

WEB EXERCISE: Evaluating Divorce Using the Internet

The following web site is described by its creators as "an electronic resource for people involved in or facing divorce." The site offers a number of featured articles about different aspects of divorce and also provides a variety of contacts that may be useful to those who are involved. Regardless of whether you have ever been divorced (or married, for that matter) or have even thought about the prospect, this web site will provide a wealth of information:

http://www.divorce-online.com/

Chapter Twelve

EDUCATION

OBJECTIVES

After reading Chapter Twelve, you should be able to provide detailed answers to the following questions:

1. What caused the expansion of education (the "schooling revolution") in the United States?
2. Do schools provide a fair and open environment for achievement and social mobility, or is inequality a part of education as a social institution? If inequality is a part of education, why is this the case?
3. Why has the overall quality of education declined in American society?
4. How does the American system of education differ from the systems in other countries?

CHAPTER REVIEW

I.   What caused the "schooling revolution" in American society?

The text examines three explanations for the dramatic expansion of formal education in twentieth-century America: schooling for industrial society, schooling for capitalism, and status competition for a *credential society*.

A. Structural functionalists hold that mass education fills the need of complex industrial societies for skilled workers, moral and social consensus, and equal opportunities. According to this view, the creation of new occupations in the early twentieth century, the influx of foreign workers to American cities and factories, the knowledge explosion of the mid-twentieth century, and widespread acceptance of egalitarian ideas all contributed to the schooling revolution. Today, schools serve five basic functions: instruction, socialization, custody and control of young people, certification, and selection.

B. Conflict theorists view mass education as having been designed by and maintained by capitalists in order to further their own goals. During the early twentieth century, schools were designed to turn immigrant and rural children into obedient workers; later the emphasis shifted to developing white-collar skills and team (or company) loyalty. Far from promoting egalitarian ideals, schools protect the status quo by using tests and other allegedly objective measures that favor youngsters of upper- and middle-class backgrounds, and by maintaining the illusion of equal opportunity. Schools produce a surplus of qualified personnel--a boon to employers.

C. A third explanation of the schooling revolution stresses status competition. Poor parents believed schooling was a route to social mobility and demanded more education for their children. As more lower-class youngsters began completing high school, more middle-class students went on to college, keeping one educational step ahead. Today, many lower-class students attend college, and many desirable jobs require a graduate or professional degree. The result is that educational *credentials* become a form of investment and serve to maintain social inequality.

II.   Does the school system in the United States provide a fair and open environment for achievement and social mobility, or is inequality a part of education as a social institution?

Has mass education opened opportunities for social mobility, as many Americans believe? The text concludes that it has not. Any number of studies have shown, first, that the higher a student's socioeconomic status, the further up the educational ladder he or she will go; and second, that equal education has not produced equal incomes for blacks, women, and other minorities. Why do youngsters from white middle- and upper- class backgrounds profit more from education than other children?

Funding schools through local taxes naturally makes some districts better equipped than others. Common sense suggests that the better the school and the better the education that children receive, the further they will go. In recent years, many poor school districts have sued to challenge school funding inequities. One proposed solution to the problem of unequal schools is *school choice*, a plan that would allow parents to choose which school their children would attend, no matter what district they lived in. Those in favor of school choice believe it would improve the incentives for education for school administrators and teachers as well as for parents and students; opponents fear that it would only increase the social stratification that already exists in schools. Some school districts have attempted to provide parents with some degree of choice through the creation of *magnet schools* (schools with a specialized focus or teaching style).

Clearly, one proposed explanation for unequal performance in school is that middle- and upper-class children attend better schools. The Coleman report, the result of a massive study designed to assess the impact of school integration published in 1966, rejected this view. Coleman found little correlation between school quality and student performance. In 1980, the National Center for Educational Statistics sponsored a large-scale study of America's high school sophomores and seniors. The survey results were analyzed in 1981, and again in 1987, by Coleman and his colleagues. These researchers discovered that on tests of vocabulary, reading, and mathematics, students from private schools performed better than those from public schools. Catholic schools were especially effective with poor and minority students. The study also noted that private school students were much more likely to enroll in college than were graduates of public schools. Coleman and his collaborators concluded that Catholic schools succeed because they are part of a community, merging people of different generations and socioeconomic backgrounds. More recently, the limited data available indicate very small differences between academic achievement of students enrolled in private versus public schools.

Recent studies suggest that teaching strategies, commitment to learning, respect for students, and consistent discipline have a positive effect on academic achievement. Continuing racial and economic segregation and tracking may have a negative impact.

Regarding the question of whether integration reduces racial inequality in education, the findings are mixed: There is no evidence that desegregation has a negative impact on white students, but neither is there evidence that desegregation, by itself, has a strong positive effect on minority students. At the same time, economic integration does seem to have an impact. Another explanation of differences in academic achievement is unequal treatment *within* schools. Three out of four American schools use some form of *tracking*: assigning students to different classes and programs on the basis of perceived ability and interests. While tracking may be positive for students with high ability, it also reinforces and perpetuates social inequality among other students.

Education is not the great equalizer many Americans would like to believe it is: As a group, white males earn about one-third more than both white women and African Americans of both sexes.

III.   Why has the overall quality of education declined in the United States?

Our educational system seems to have reached a crisis point. The deteriorating physical condition of inner-city schools is well documented, and violence in schools is another issue of growing concern. Standardized tests show that student performance in the United States is declining for the most part and that American students are only average when compared with their counterparts in other industrialized nations. A number of critics blame reduced standards for the decline in achievement by American students. The quality and supply of elementary and secondary school teachers is another cause for concern. Surprisingly, students are "passively content" with what goes on in classrooms. The other side of the coin is that teachers are being asked to do more and more in the classroom while being given fewer resources with which to accomplish their goals. Undoubtedly, the most alarming educational information to come to light in the 1980s was the number of adult Americans who could not read or write. Illiteracy is expensive, for individuals and for societies, and critics of our educational system see this problem as only the "tip of the iceberg." Would national standards interfere with local control? This issue is extremely controversial, with most of the criticism coming from educators: Who, critics ask, would decide what students should know? Some of the more controversial recommendations concern the training and evaluation of teachers. Observers have questioned the costs and benefits of professionalizing teaching; virtually everyone agrees that finding ways of improving the professionalization, pay, and status of teachers is crucial to improving the quality of education, but the question is *how* to achieve these goals.

Many people see equal education for disadvantaged children as the major challenge of the 1990s and the twenty-first century. Study after study has shown that poor and minority children are at risk. This raises another question: How can America strive for educational excellence for all students, including the increasing number of disadvantaged youths?

IV.   How does the American system of education differ from equivalent systems in other countries?

Cross-cultural comparisons help identify the unique features of the American system of education. The American educational system emphasizes individual ability and achievement, in comparison to an emphasis on group achievement in Communist societies like China. Americans believe in equal education for all (contest mobility), in contrast to western Europe, where higher education has been viewed traditionally as a privilege for the upper classes or for those of unusual ability (sponsored mobility). In Japan, the educational system is structured like a pyramid, with broad-based elementary education, a narrower selection of academic high schools, and a very small number of elite universities at the top. In Japan, children are viewed as full-time scholars, in contrast to the American view, wherein young people are also supposed to "have fun" growing up. Japan has an impressive record in terms of academic achievement, but this system depends upon sacrifices few Americans are prepared to make.

CONCEPT REVIEW

Match each of the following terms with the correct definition:

a. education (p. 444)
b. schooling (p. 444)
c. tracking (p. 459)
d. status competition (p. 452)
e. structural-functionalist per-
     spective (p. 445)
f. conflict perspective
     (p. 449)

g. magnet schools (p. 468)
h. self-fulfilling prophecies
     (p. 461)
i. school choice (p. 468)
j. ideal culture (p. 473)
k. real culture (p. 473)

1.___ Formal instruction in a classroom setting.
2.___ The quest for prestige and social esteem.
3.___ The formal or informal transmission of knowledge and skills.
4.___ The perspective maintaining that education expanded to meet the demands of an increasingly complex, industrialized society.
5.___ Assigning students to different classes or programs on the basis of test scores and teacher perceptions.
6.___ The perspective maintaining that public schools were designed primarily to instill the qualities industrialists wanted in their workers.
7.___ A plan that allows parents to select which school their children may attend, no matter what district they live in.
8.___ Schools with a specialized focus or teaching style.

9.___ False predictions that influence behavior in such a way that the predictions come true.

10.___ Norms and values that people may not formally admit to, but practice nonetheless.

11.___ Norms and values to which people openly and formally adhere.

Answers

1.	b	5.	c	9.	h
2.	d	6.	f	10.	k
3.	a	7.	i	11.	j
4.	e	8.	g		

REVIEW QUESTIONS

1. When the president of a college awards diplomas on graduation day, which function of education is being served?
   a. instruction
   b. socialization
   c. certification
   d. selection

2. In preindustrial America, which of the following institutions was responsible for the education of children?
   a. the family
   b. the church
   c. the school
   d. all of the above

3. The theory of status competition advanced by Hurn differs from other views of the schooling revolution in that it:
   a. views mass education as functional
   b. views mass education as dysfunctional
   c. traces the schooling revolution to the vested interests of educators
   d. traces the schooling revolution to the hopes and dreams of parents for their child.

4.   Which theoretical view holds that one of the consequences of the schooling revolution is to create an oversupply of trained personnel?
     a.   structural functionalism
     b.   conflict theory
     c.   status competition
     d.   sponsored mobility

5.   According to the text's discussion of educational stratification in Russia:
     a.   under the old tsarist regime, education was open to the members of all social classes
     b.   after the Russian revolution of 1917, the new communist regime launched a campaign to end illiteracy.
     c.   in the years leading up to World War II, enrollment in primary and secondary schools declined to a new, all-time low.
     d.   none of the above

6.   According to Christopher Hurn, an alternative explanation for the schooling revolution is the quest for prestige and social esteem, or:
     a.   credentialing
     b.   tracking
     c.   status competition
     d.   sponsored mobility

7.   According to the research conducted by Sewell and his colleagues concerning the relationship between socioeconomic status and academic achievement:
     a.   social class has no effect on students' achievements
     b.   social class has strong effects on students' achievements
     c.   children from lower-class homes do as well in school as those from upper-class families
     d.   students from upper-class families are equally as likely to obtain a graduate-level education as their lower-class counterparts

8.   The primary source of funding for local school districts is:
     a.   private donations
     b.   state income taxes
     c.   the local property tax
     d.   a equal combination of all of the above

9. Studies of the impact of school integration show that:
   a. minority students placed in classrooms with a majority of middle- to upper-class students show substantial gains in academic achievement
   b. desegregation has strong, positive effects on minority students
   c. desegregation has a negative impact on white students.
   d. none of the above

10. According to the text's discussion of tracking:
    a. one out of four American schools use some form of tracking
    b. advocates and critics alike agree that all students benefit from tracking
    c. tracking may be good for students with high ability
    d. tracking has headed off resegregation

11. The boxed insert entitled *Pygmalion in the Classroom* exemplifies:
    a. *My Fair Lady*
    b. tracking
    c. desegregation of schools
    d. none of the above

12. According to the text's discussion of race, gender, and academic achievement:
    a. education is the great equalizer
    b. male-female differences in math test scores are increasing
    c. as a group, white males earn about one-third more than both white women and African Americans of both sexes
    d. African Americans have the highest percentage of high school dropouts nationwide

13. According to the text's discussion of student achievement:
    a. American students are significantly above the average when compared with their counterparts in other industrialized nations
    b. SAT results refer to all high school students
    c. the more television students watch, the higher their SAT scores
    d. student performance in the United States is declining for the most part

14. In 1996, by a margin of 54 percent, Californians approved *Proposition 209.* This controversial piece of legislation:
    a. guaranteed the application of affirmative action policies in the state
    b. prohibited the use of racial or gender preferences in hiring, contracting, and education
    c. approved gender preferences in hiring, contracting, and education, but suspended racially-based preferences
    d. approved racial preferences in hiring, contracting, and education, but suspended gender-based preferences

15. According to the text, the most alarming educational information to come to light in the 1980s was:
    a. the number of adult Americans who cannot read or write
    b. the ongoing amount of segregation in America's school systems
    c. the drop in SAT scores
    d. the high school drop-out rate

16. Which of the following is NOT one of the policy debates surrounding school reform?
    a. the creation of national standards for elementary and secondary education
    b. national certification for teachers
    c. whether to assist disadvantaged children
    d. magnet schools and vouchers

17. In the People's Republic of China:
    a. the curriculum focuses on moral education
    b. individuality is greatly emphasized
    c. children are taught to place the needs of the state and the group above their own
    d. a and c above

18.   According to the text's discussion of American and European educational systems:
    a.   Europe displays a system of contest mobility
    b.   the American educational system is one of sponsored mobility
    c.   both contest and sponsored mobility systems are "pure types"
    d.   none of the above

19.   According to the text's discussion of education in Western Europe:
    a.   occupational status in the United States usually reflects the number of years a person has remained in school
    b.   today, secondary education in Britain is very different than it is in America
    c.   in general, European universities have higher standards off instruction and offer this opportunity to a larger segment of the population in comparison with American institutions
    d.   none of the above

20.   According to the text's discussion of education in Japan:
    a.   Americans tend to have higher standards for performance than the Japanese
    b.   the Japanese believe that all children are born equal and that there is no ceiling on achievement, in contrast to Americans, who think of each child as a unique individual and attribute success in school to a combination of innate or inherited ability and opportunity
    c.   American students work much harder in comparison with Japanese students
    d.   none of the above

Answers

1.   c: One of the functions of education is to verify that individuals have met certain standards. (Schooling for Industrial Society; p. 447)
2.   d: But the family, followed by the church, held primary responsibility for teaching values and skills; school was a luxury. (The Schooling Revolution: Three Interpretations; p. 445)

3. d: In Hurn's view, education has become a status symbol. Much as Americans used to compete with their neighbors over who owned the biggest car, so they compete over whose children have the most education. Hurn is neutral on the question of whether the schooling revolution is functional. (Schooling for Capitalism; p. 452)

4. b: According to conflict theory, the *capitalist elite* uses the education system to serve its own interests--in this case, being able to offer lower wages because there are more people seeking jobs than there are jobs available. (Schooling for Capitalism; p. 449)

5. b: Under the old tsarist regime, education was a privilege reserved for Russia's elite and in the years leading up to World War II, enrollment in primary and secondary schools soared. (A Global View: Educational Stratification in Russia; pp. 450-451)

6. c: Credentialing refers to the process whereby society specifies certain degrees and regimens of experience required to occupy particular job positions; tracking refers to assigning students to different classes or programs on the basis of test scores and teacher perceptions; and sponsored mobility refers to a system in which certain people are identified as destined for particular positions. (Status Competition and Credentials; p. 452)

7. b: Regardless of the measure of socioeconomic status employed, children from lower-class homes do not do as well in school as those from upper-class homes; social class has strong effects on students' achievements. (Unequal Schools; p. 454)

8. c: Since wealthy communities tend to have higher property tax rates than poorer towns, schools in well-off districts have more money. (Unequal Schools; p. 456)

9. a: Does integration reduce racial inequality in education? The findings are mixed: There is no evidence that desegregation has a negative impact on white students, but neither is there evidence that desegregation, by itself, has a strong, positive effect on minority students. Economic integration does seem to have an impact. (School Resegregation?; p. 459)

10. c: Three out of four American schools use some form of tracking; only those advocates of tracking feel that the process benefits *all* students; tracking has led to resegregation, especially in inner-city schools; but tracking may be good for students with high ability.

(Tracking; pp. 459-461)

11.   b: Tracking provides an example of how the "Pygmalion effect" can influence a child's academic achievement. ("Closeup": Pygmalion in the Classroom; p. 461)

12.   c: Education is not the great equalizer many Americans would like to believe it is, and although the effects of social class can account for many of the inequities found among racial and ethnic minorities and among women, two other powerful influences are racism and sexism. (Race, Gender, and Academic Achievement; pp. 455-456)

13.   d: Standardized tests show that student performance is declining for the most part. SAT results refer only to those high school students who plan to go to college; watching television takes time away from other activities that stimulate student achievement; American students are only average when compared to their counterparts in other industrialized nations. (Student Achievement; pp. 463-464)

14.   b: Proposition 209 prohibited the use of racial or gender preferences in hiring, contracting, and education. (Affirmative Action; p. 472)

15.   a: The United States ranks an embarrassing forty-ninth among the 158 members of the United Nations in literacy. (Illiterate? Who, US?; p. 466)

16.   c: Educators do know a number of ways to help disadvantaged children take advantage of education, and people generally support this notion, but whether educators will be given the resources to implement these programs is another matter. (School Reform: The Policy Debates; pp. 466; 468-472)

17.   d: China attempts to further socialism through education, placing special emphasis on the needs of the group or the state. This is in direct contrast to the American system, which stresses individuality. (Education in China; pp. 473-476)

18.   d: The United States illustrates a system of contest mobility in contrast to the European system, which illustrates sponsored mobility; neither of these education systems is a "pure type." (Education in Western Europe; p. 476)

19.   a: Occupational status in the United States usually reflects the number of years a person has remained in school, whereas occupational status in Britain and Germany usually reflects the

type of school a person has attended; today, secondary education in Britain resembles that in America; in general, European universities have higher standards of instruction, but offer this opportunity to a smaller segment of the population. (Education in Western Europe; 476-477)

20. b: The Japanese do not stress the unique individuality of children, as Americans do, but emphasize that with hard work, there are no limits to what children may achieve; the Japanese tend to have higher standards of performance than Americans do; and Japanese students work much harder than American students do. (Education in Japan; 477-479)

CRITICAL THINKING

1. The United States has often been referred to as the "credentialed society." Do you think Americans place too much emphasis on educational credentials? What if a person already knows how to do a job well, but lacks a formal degree--should he/she be hired? Why or why not?

2. Discuss with your classmates your different motivations for attending college and the various difficulties you experienced in doing so. How do these motivations and difficulties vary according to the social background of you and your peers?

WEB EXERCISE: Affirmative Action--Pro and Con

The text's discussion of this topic provides a glimpse of the controversy that surrounds this very explosive social issue. On the World Wide Web, the discussion of this controversy is mirrored in a huge reservoir of sites and resources. The following address offers access to these locations:

http://www.ahandyguide.com

Upon accessing the main page, look for "search engines" and click on this feature. Then, type in "affirmative action." This will bring up a screen where numerous sites are listed that deal with affirmative action issues. If you want to learn more about the issues, the general, informational sites are your best bet. Then, you may wish to proceed to evaluating the "pros" and "cons" via sites that obviously take one point of view versus the other.

Chapter Thirteen

RELIGION

OBJECTIVES

After reading Chapter Thirteen, you should be able to provide detailed answers to the following questions:

1. What are the basic elements of religion? Why is some form of religion found in all human societies?
2. How do sociologists explain the relationship between religion and society?
3. What are the different types of religious organizations, and what distinguishes them?
4. What central dilemma do all religious organizations face?
5. How has the role of religion changed in contemporary society? How has religious life changed in the United States during the 1990s?

CHAPTER REVIEW

I. What are the basic elements of religion?

Although the contents vary enormously, all societies have some form of *religion*: any set of institutionalized beliefs and practices that deal with the ultimate meaning of life. Religion fills the gap between human aspirations and abilities; between social expectations and experiences; and between the ambiguities of life and the need to understand.

The text identifies four basic elements of religion. Religious *beliefs* are ideas about a divine or supernatural order that organize people's perceptions of events. Religious *rituals* are symbolic representations of beliefs and events that confirm this supernatural order. *Subjective experiences* are inner feelings that reveal or confirm one's faith. The fourth element of religion is a *community* of believers who share this faith.

II.   **How have sociologists explained the link between religion and society?**

Sociologists have offered three different views of the relationship between society and religion.

A. Durkheim began with the observation that all societies distinguish between the *sacred* (or holy) and the *profane* (or ordinary). In the simplest societies, people treat the totem that is associated with their clan with awe. *Totemic* religions illustrate how all religions reflect social forces and thus serve as a celebration of the social order. Durkheim argued that religion gives concrete expression to our unconscious awareness of social forces; that the function of religion in society is to establish a moral community and reinforce social solidarity through community rituals. He held that if religions as we know them were to disappear, some *functional equivalent* would arise to replace them.

B. In contrast, Marx stressed the oppressive qualities of religion. In an often-quoted passage, he characterized religion as the *opium of the people*. By this, he meant that religion lulls the masses into inaction by preaching that existing social conditions are divinely ordained or that suffering in this world will be rewarded in the next.

C. While Marx saw religion as an obstacle to social change, Weber saw it as an *agent* of change. Weber puzzled over why the leading capitalists of the day were overwhelmingly Protestant--why weren't these leaders Catholic, or Buddhist, or Muslim? He found an answer in the Calvinist phase of the Protestant Reformation. Calvin believed that the individual's fate in the hereafter is preordained, but he did not advocate passive acceptance of whatever life brought. Rather, he preached the redemptive value of work. The Protestant work ethic, with its peculiar combination of hard work and deferred gratification, was ideally suited to capitalism. Under Calvinism, investing in profit-making ventures became a moral duty. In this case, then, religion played a major, active role in social change.

III.   **What are the different types of religious organizations, and what distinguishes them?**

Religions are organizations as well as sets of beliefs. The text identifies four distinct types of religious organizations:
A.   An *established church* is a state religion, which supports and is supported by the existing social structure; it is accepted by most members of society as the *one true faith*. The term *church* applies to any state religion, Christian or non-Christian.
B. A *sect* also claims to be the one true religion, but unlike an established church, a sect opposes the existing social structure and may withdraw from society or actively attack established institutions.
C. A *denomination* is a religious organization that accepts the social order and also accepts the existence and legitimacy of other religions. Unlike the established church and sect, it does not claim to hold the only key to salvation.
D. In everyday conversation, the term *sect* is often used interchangeably with *cult*, but sociologists use the latter term to describe a loosely organized religion that opposes the existing social structure, but focuses on changing the individual rather than the established social order.

IV.   **What central dilemma do all religious organizations face?**

As shown in this typology, the relationship between religion and social structure in modern societies is extremely variable. The same religion may be a sect in one society, but an established church or denomination in another. All religions must, at some point, face the dilemma of institutionalization. In becoming established (attracting members, creating symbols, developing organization, etc.), the religion's original values and goals are distorted and may be abandoned. O'Dea identified five dilemmas of religious organizations: mixed motivations, challenges to the symbol system, organization, letter versus the spirit of religious law, and conversion versus coercion.

V.   **How has the role of religion changed in contemporary society? How has religious life changed in the United States during the 1990s?**

Most sociologists agree that the trend toward *secularization* (the removal of religious control over social life) is undeniable, but they disagree about what this trend means.

Some believe that religion is dying, that it has been reduced to the status of a hobby. Weber was one of the strongest critics of secularization; he saw secularization as part of an overall trend toward rationalization in modern societies.

Others argue that although religion is changing, it is not disappearing. Bellah sees the emphasis on personal autonomy as the defining characteristic of modern religion. People are less inclined to accept the teachings of their religion without question or to expect prayer to solve social problems. Bellah sees this as the product of religious evolution (from primitive to archaic, historic, and early modern religion). He also sees *civil religion* (the belief that a nation has a special relationship with God) as evidence of the continuing need for sacred symbols.

Even though there are thousands of different religions being practiced around the world, religion's standing as a social institution becomes clear when one considers that over three quarters of the world population belong to one of six major religions: Buddhism, Christianity, Confucianism, Hinduism, Islam, and Judaism.

VI.   How has the role of religion changed in modern society, and how is religious life changing in the United States during the 1990s?

The United States is one of the most "religious" nations in the western industrial world: Two out of three Americans are now or were "churched," that is, they are either members of a church or synagogue or attended services in the last six months, not counting holidays. Polls indicate that the vast majority of Americans hold traditional beliefs. Interest and confidence in religion dropped sharply during the 1960s and 1970s, but then began to recover.

Religious participation in the U.S. today is characterized by two apparently contradictory trends: A majority of Americans hold traditional religious beliefs, and many are members of churches or synagogues. On the other hand, less than 42 percent of those same persons polled said they attended services in the last week. Many sociologists believe this to be the result of the *privatization* of religion. Americans draw a distinction between their personal relationship with God and participation in a religious organization.

Religious life in America has been seen to change since World War II. Sociologist Robert Wuthnow has surveyed religious life in America over the past four decades, and has concluded that the nature of religion has changed *radically*. In the 1940s, religion was primarily centered around neighborhood churches. People achieved a large part of their identities based on their membership in a religious denomination. Church and government had a relaxed, alliance-type relationship. Fundamentalism resurfaced after World War II. By the 1980s, television ministry had become as important as the neighborhood church, and the religious "right" became powerfully mobilized. Peoples' identities began to be derived more from where they stood on social issues than from their membership in a particular denomination; and religion had become an outspoken voice in American politics.

These trends have had a *polarizing* effect on religion in America: Boundaries between denominations have been blurred as members of many different religions routinely join forces in opposition or support on social issues. Religion has become issue-oriented and, as a result, is often in the forefront of political debates.

CONCEPT REVIEW

Match each of the following items with the correct definition:

a.   cult (p. 492)   g.   established church (p. 491)
b.   ritual (p. 486)   h.   belief (p. 485)
c.   secularization (p. 496)   i.   civil religion (p. 499)
d.   totem (p. 487)   j.   profane (p. 487)
e.   religion (p. 484)   k.   sect (p. 491)
f.   denomination (p. 491)   l.   sacred (p. 487)

1.___   A conviction that cannot be proved or disproved by ordinary means.
2.___   A set of beliefs, rituals, and symbols that define a nation's special relationship with God.
3.___   Ordinary, everyday things that may be treated casually.
4.___   That which is holy, inspires awe, and must be treated with respect.
5.___   A religious organization that asserts its unique legitimacy but stands apart from society.
6.___   Any set of institutionalized beliefs and practices that deal with the ultimate meaning of life.
7.___   The official religion of its society.
8.___   A sacred emblem that members of a group or clan treat with reverence and awe.

9.___ The removal of religious control over social life.
10.___ A religious organization that accepts the legitimacy of other religions but has a negative relationship with society.
11.___ A formalized, stylized enactment of religious beliefs.
12.___ A religious organization that has a positive relationship to society and accepts the legitimacy of other religions.

Answers

1.	h	7.	g
2.	i	8.	d
3.	j	9.	c
4.	l	10.	a
5.	k	11.	b
6.	e	12.	f

REVIEW QUESTIONS

1. Which of the following is NOT one of the four basic elements of religion?
   a. beliefs
   b. rituals
   c. bureaucracy
   d. subjective experiences

2. Which of the following theorists viewed religion as an agent of social change?
   a. Emile Durkheim
   b. Karl Marx
   c. Max Weber
   d. none of the above

3. Religious beliefs differ from other kinds of beliefs in that they:
    a. deal with intangibles
    b. attempt to explain the meaning of life
    c. influence and are influenced by the society in which the religion is found
    d. are based on faith in powers and processes that cannot be proved by simple observation

4. According to the text's discussion of *totems*:
    a. the things chosen as totems are awe-inspiring in and of themselves
    b. a totem is a symbol of the clan, but not a symbol of god
    c. a lizard, a caterpillar, a fish, or a tree might be totems
    d. all of the above

5. Durkheim maintained that all societies:
    a. have some form of totem
    b. distinguish between the sacred and the profane
    c. worship in the same ways
    d. hold primitive beliefs about social forces

6. Weber held that the Protestant work ethic:
    a. was responsible for the rise of capitalism
    b. contributed to the rise of capitalism
    c. was a by-product of the rise of capitalism
    d. disproved Marx's economic view of history

7. The principal difference between a sect and a cult is that:
    a. a sect accepts the existing social order
    b. a cult accepts the existing social order
    c. a sect accepts the legitimacy of other religions
    d. a cult focuses on individual salvation rather than on social change

8.   In what place and time would the Roman Catholic Church be classified as a denomination?
   a.   the Roman Empire
   b.   medieval Europe
   c.   the United States today
   d.   Italy today

9.   Which of the following theorists saw contemporary religion as the ultimate cause of alienation?
   a.   Emile Durkheim
   b.   Karl Marx
   c.   Max Weber
   d.   Robert Bellah

10.   In seeking to establish itself, a religion may admit members with mixed motivations. This illustrates:
   a.   the dilemmas of institutionalization
   b.   secularization
   c.   the dysfunctions of religion
   d.   all of the above

11.   According to sociologist Max Weber:
   a.   changes in the relationship between religion and society are evidence of decline
   b.   secularization is part of an overall trend toward rationalization in modern societies
   c.   the result of rationalization is "disenchantment."
   d.   all of the above

12.   Which of the following is NOT one of O'Dea's dilemmas of religious organizations?
   a.   obtaining new members
   b.   mixed motivations
   c.   letter versus the spirit of religious law
   d.   conversion versus coercion

13. Which of the following is NOT one of Bellah's types of religions in the process of religious evolution?
    a. primitive religion
    b. archaic religion
    c. totemic religion
    d. early modern religion

14. Which of the following is NOT one of the six major religious discussed in the text?
    a. Buddhism
    b. Confucianism
    c. Islam
    d. Televangelism

15. Who called religion the *opium of the people*?
    a. Max Weber
    b. Karl Marx
    c. Emile Durkheim
    d. Robert Bellah

16. All religions share which of the following characteristics?
    a. a quest for visions and mystical experiences
    b. rituals that symbolize beliefs
    c. a belief in spirits
    d. a belief in God

17. Which of the following is an example of secularization?
    a. religious sponsorship of political campaigns and social movements (such as the *right-to-life* movement)
    b. an ecumenical council whose members are meeting to debate the issue of a nuclear freeze
    c. the ruling against prayers in public schools
    d. TV evangelism

18.   When the Puritans rebelled against the pomp and ceremony of the
        Anglican Church and set sail for the New World to find a *society of saints*,
        they were:
        a.   an established church
        b.   a sect
        c.   a denomination
        d.   a cult

19.   Although it would be an exaggeration to say that the United States
        experienced a religious revival, the 1980s witnessed an increase in:
        a.   church attendance
        b.   the belief in God
        c.   overall agreement that religion is very important
        d.   cult membership

20.   The new televangelists differed from evangelist and mainstream ministers
        in which of the following ways?
        a.   Nearly all of the new televangelists were headquartered on the
                West Coast.
        b.   The new televangelists were unwilling to be associated with "that
                old-time religion."
        c.   The new televangelists refused to preach a literal interpretation
                of the Bible.
        d.   None of the above

Answers

1.   c: The religious framework is composed of four basic elements:
                beliefs, rituals, subjective experience, and community. (The
                Elements of Religion; p. 485)
2.   c: Weber's prime example was the Protestant Reformation, as
                linked to the establishment of the work ethic and the spread of
                capitalism. (Religion and Society: Three Views; pp. 489-490)
3.   d: People may believe in God and also in modern medicine,
                sociological analysis, and the wisdom of Plato. The difference
                between religious beliefs and other types of beliefs is that the
                latter can be proved or disproved by observation or logic. Faith,

on the other hand, is, by definition, belief without question. (The Elements of Religion; p. 486)

4.   c: The things chosen as totems (a lizard, a caterpillar, a fish, a tree) are not, in themselves, awe-inspiring. A totem is both a symbol of god and a symbol of the clan. (The Sacred, the Profane, and the Collective: Durkheim; p. 487)

5.   b: Religious beliefs and practices may vary, but the idea that some things (objects, places, people, days) are holy and should be treated with reverence is universal. The question for Durkheim was *why?* His answer was that religion functions to create and maintain a moral community. (The Sacred, the Profane, and the Collective: Durkheim; p. 487)

6.   b: Weber saw the Protestant work ethic as one of many factors in the rise of capitalism. His goal was not to prove Marx wrong, but to show that one-dimensional explanations of social change are simplistic. (Religion and Society: Three Views; pp. 489-490)

7.   d: Cults are more loosely organized, more transient, and more individualistic than sects. They focus on the salvation of the individual cult members. (Types of Religious Organizations; pp. 491-492)

8.   c: A denomination is a religious organization that is not affiliated with the state and coexists with other religions. Although Italy is not a religious state per se, the overwhelming majority of the population is Catholic, and the Catholic Church influences most areas of public and private life. (Types of Religious Organizations; p. 492)

9.   b: Whereas Durkheim held that religion reduces alienation by linking individuals to a moral community, Marx argued that religion creates alienation by denying that human beings are responsible for social injustices. (Religion and Society: Three Views; p. 488)

10.   a: The original members of a religion may be wholeheartedly dedicated to its values, beliefs, and practices. If it seeks to expand, however, a religion may have to admit members who are as interested in making social contacts, in gaining prestige, or in some other personal ambition as they are in the religion itself. (The Dilemmas of Institutionalization; pp. 493; 496)

11.   d: According to Weber, changes in the relationship between religion

and society reflected evidence of societal decline; secularization is part of an overall trend toward rationalization in modern societies; and the result of rationalization, in Weber's words, is disenchantment. (The Trend Toward Secularization; pp. 489-490)

12.   a: O'Dea's central point is that institutionalization is necessary if a religion is to pursue its original goals. The five basic dilemmas are: mixed motivations, challenges to the religion's symbol system, organization, letter versus the spirit of religious law, and conversion versus coercion. (The Dilemmas of Institutionalization; pp. 493; 496)

13.   c: Durkheim spoke of totemic religion; Bellah specified the following forms of religion as the evolutionary process moves from simple to more complex: primitive religion, archaic religion, historic religion, early modern religion, and modern religion. (The Trend Toward Secularization; pp. 497-499)

14.   d: The six major wold religious are Buddhism, Christianity, Confucianism, Hinduism, Islam, and Judaism. (World Religions; p. 500)

15.   b: Marx held that religion supports the existing system of social stratification by declaring that all life follows a divine plan, denying the role humans play in social institutions, and thus, lulling the masses into passive acceptance of the status quo. (Religion and Society: Three Views; p. 488)

16.   b: All religions use rituals to recall and reinforce sacred beliefs. The other answers apply to some, but not all, religions. (The Elements of Religion; pp. 485-486)

17.   c: Secularization refers not to the involvement of religion in public affairs, but to the reverse--removing religion from public affairs (in this case, education). (The Trend Toward Secularization; pp. 496-497)

18.   b: In rejecting the Church of England, the Puritans were a sect. Once they arrived in the New World and established their own communities, however, they became a church. (Types of Religious Organizations; p. 491)

19.   c: Oddly, the percentage of people who say religion is very important has increased in recent years, but church attendance has not. (Religion in the U.S.: An Overview; p. 505)

20.   d: Nearly all of the new televangelists were headquartered in the

South; they were eager to be associated with fundamentalism, and they preached a literal interpretation of the Bible. (The Restructuring of Religion in America; p. 509)

CRITICAL THINKING

1. Religion in American society tends to be *monotheistic* (one god or deity). Do any of the practices of mainstream religions seem to reflect *polytheistic* (more than one god) practices? How about religions of "the way" (religions based on immutable truths that reveal the proper way to achieve fulfillment rather than the existence of deities)?

2. Do you think religion in American society will become more or less important in the future? Do events suggest that secularization is becoming more widespread or less? Do any practices at your college or university seem to indicate the existence of a *civil religion*?

WEB EXERCISE: Cults and the Internet

In the aftermath of the "Heaven's Gate" mass-suicide incident, there has been increased concern about various cults seeking membership using the Internet. The following site will provide you with a stepping-off place for learning more about cults, both in reference to the Internet as well as in general. From this site, a number of interesting links are provided that will enable you to obtain even more information about cults.

http://www.sd83.bc.ca/stu/9711/hah2-3.html

Chapter Fourteen

POLITICS

OBJECTIVES

After reading Chapter Fourteen, you should be able to provide detailed answers to the following questions:

1. What is the difference between power and authority?
2. How has the development of modern political institutions affected the distribution of authority?
3. What are the basic elements of the American political system?
4. Who actually rules America today?
5. How do political systems vary around the world?

CHAPTER REVIEW

I.   What is the difference between power and authority?

Politics refers to the social processes by which people gain, use, and lose power, and it plays an important role in virtually all human relationships.

Power is the ability to control what other people do, even when they resist. *Authority* refers to the legitimate use of power. Virtually all political systems depend on a combination of authority and coercion, but no government can rule through force alone. One of the central functions of political institutions is to legitimate the ways in which power is exercised in society. Weber identified three main sources of political legitimacy: *Traditional authority* is based on customs handed down through the generations; *Charismatic authority* is based on special personal qualities; *Rational-legal authority* derives from a formal system of rules or laws. All three of these types of authority are "ideal types," or abstractions of key characteristics.

II. How has the development of modern political institutions affected the distribution of authority?

One of the defining characteristics of modern societies is the development of specialized political institutions: courts, legislatures, political parties, government agencies, a military, and an executive branch of government. Together, these entities make up what sociologists call "the state." The first stage in the development of states was the separation of the office of king from the person who was king. But kingdoms were loose alliances of principalities, not nations in the modern sense of the word. The second stage in the development of states involved the drawing of national boundaries and the creation of public bureaucracies. In Europe, these developments occurred because the expansion of capitalism made rules based on traditional loyalties obsolete.

In the twentieth century, the size and scope of the state increased dramatically. This expansion of government activities and authority led to the evolution of a *welfare state*, in which the government assumes varying degrees of responsibility for the well-being of citizens. One consequence of adoption of welfare state principles was enormous growth of federal bureaucracy. Another major theme in modern history is the expansion in people's ideas of their rights. Whereas traditional political systems assign people different rights on the basis of kinship, gender, and age, modern rational-legal political systems usually ascribe the same basic rights to all (or most) citizens. In the second half of the twentieth century, the concept of human rights, rights that override any political or social system, gained at least verbal acceptance.

III. What are the basic elements of the American political system?

The political system of the United States is based on the ideal of democracy and emphasizes four main points: the importance of the individual, consent of the governed, majority rules and minority rights, and equality of opportunity. One of the distinguishing features of American democracy is the *separation of powers*. Two traditional forms of political participation are voting and political parties. Interest groups, political action committees (PACs), and protest movements are also involved.

In the United States today, we consider the principle of "one person, one vote" a cornerstone of democracy, but this was not always the case. In practice, few Americans take advantage of their basic right to vote. One reason voter turnout in the U.S. is low may be obstacles to voter registration. Low voter turnout may be an expression of apathy and alienation from the political system.

A *political party* is a collectivity organized to gain and hold legitimate control of government. Party politics in this country is shaped by the fact that our political system is a *presidential democracy*, in which the executive and legislative branches of government are separate. Political parties in the United States are loosely organized coalitions of national, state, and local groups. In the *parliamentary democracies* of Europe and Asia, people do not vote directly for the head of state, but minority parties can have a significant impact. Unlike most other democracies, the United States has only two major political parties. Third parties have had some impact at the state and local level, but rarely at the national level. Increasingly, politics in the U.S. has become less party-oriented and more issue-oriented. Likewise, American voters have become more issue-oriented.

An *interest group* is an organization created to pressure public officials to make decisions that will benefit their members or promote a particular cause. One of the most powerful and successful pressure groups in the United States is the National Rifle Association. Interest groups derive power from two main sources: information and money. The most direct and effective way of influencing elected officials is through campaign contributions. *Political action committees (PACs)* are organizations formed by interest groups to collect small contributions from large numbers of people to be donated to candidates who support their particular cause or position. Television advertising plays a key, if not deciding, role in U.S. elections at all levels. Critics argue that PACs have undermined the goals of campaign reform, while supporters feel that they perform useful functions.

A *protest movement* is a grass-roots effort to change established policies and practices. Protest movements mobilize people who either had not been aware of an issue or had not had the power or organization to make themselves heard. Protest movements may be narrowly self-interested, concerned with only a minor reform, or they may be radical in their aims, seeking fundamental changes in existing institutions.

IV.   Who actually rules in America today?

Sociologists have proposed four different models of the structure of power in the United States. *Pluralists* describe a complex pattern of criss-crossing interest groups, which prevents the concentration of power in the hands of a single group but may also lead to paralysis. Mills and others believed that real authority lies in a *power elite*, composed of decision makers in the executive branch of government, the military, and large corporations. Domhoff and the *instrumental-ists* argue that a national upper class is in control. *Structuralists*, on the other hand, hold that policies and plans are based on the needs of the capitalist system.

V.   How do political systems vary around the world?

Political systems can be divided in two broad categories: In *authoritarian political systems*, the state claims an exclusive right to exercise political power and ordinary people are denied the right to participate in government. The three main types of authoritarian rule are *monarchy*, in which one person inherits the right to be head of state; *dictatorship*, in which one person assumes authoritarian rule but does not enjoy traditional authority; and *totalitarian states*, in which the ruling party not only controls the government, but also regulates social, economic, intellectual, cultural, and spiritual activities.

In a *democracy*, citizens have the right to run or at least to choose their own government. In a *direct democracy*, all citizens gather to debate and vote on the issues at hand; in a *representative democracy*, citizens elect representatives who set policies and enact laws in the people's name. The legitimacy of government officials rests on the support they receive in elections. The United States has a representative democratic system. In practice, no political system is purely authoritarian or democratic. Equally important, politics is now a global affair. The exercise of power, whether internally or internationally, is shaped by structural forces that are beyond the control of any one government or nation.

CONCEPT REVIEW

Match each of the following terms with the correct definition.

a.   political party (p. 527)
b.   authority (p. 517)
c.   direct democracy (p. 543)
d.   authoritarian
     political systems (p. 538)
e.   state (p. 520)
f.   democracy (p. 543)
g.   interest group (p. 530)
h.   welfare state (p. 523)

i.   political action
     committees (PACS)
     (p. 533)
j.   rational-legal
     authority (p. 519)
k.   power (p. 517)
l.   protest movement (p. 534)
m.   charismatic
     authority (p. 519)

n.   politics (p. 517)   p.   traditional
o.   totalitarianism (p. 541)   authority (p. 519)
                                          q.   representative democracy
                                                 (p. 544)

1.___   The ability to control what others do, even when they resist.
2.___   A collectivity organized to gain and hold legitimate control of govern-
        ment.
3.___   Authority that is based on customs handed down through the genera-
        tions.
4.___   The specialized institutions and organizations that have a monopoly over
        the use of force in a given territory.
5.___   Organizations formed by interest groups to collect small contributions
        from large numbers of people to be donated to candidates who support
        their particular cause or position.
6.___   A political system in which the ruling party not only controls the
        government, but also regulates most activities.
7.___   A political system in which the state claims an exclusive right to exercise
        political power and ordinary people are denied the right to participate in
        government.
8.___   Authority based on special personal qualities.
9.___   A political system in which citizens have the right to run or at least
        choose their own government.
10.___ The social processes whereby people gain, use, or lose power.
11.___ A state in which the government assumes varying degrees of responsibil-
        ity for the well-being of citizens.
12.___ A political system in which citizens run their own government.
13.___ The legitimate use of power
14.___ An organization created to pressure public officials to make decisions that
        will benefit their members or promote a particular cause.
15.___ A grass-roots effort to change established policies and practices.
16.___ Authority that derives from a formal system of rules or laws.
17.___ A political system in which citizens elect representatives who set policies
        and enact laws in the people's name.

Answers

1.	k	7.	d	13.	b
2.	a	8.	m	14.	g
3.	p	9.	f	15.	l
4.	e	10.	n	16.	j
5.	i	11.	h	17.	q
6.	o	12.	c		

REVIEW QUESTIONS

1. Which of the following best illustrates *power*?
   a. A government requires its citizens to pay income taxes
   b. A politician demands a bribe from a person who depends upon her for support
   c. Congress votes to commit the nation to war
   d. All of the above are examples of power.

2. Which of the following illustrates the exercise of authority as the text defines the term?
   a. A father beats his son with a whip after finding out that the boy stole candy from a local store.
   b. A group of protestors interferes with the construction of a nuclear power plant.
   c. The Vietnamese army assists the government of Cambodia in suppressing internal rebellions.
   d. The president of a company fires an employee who he feels is unproductive.

3. A king or queen, an emperor or tribal chief, commanding his or her subjects, exemplifies _____ authority.
   a. traditional
   b. charismatic
   c. rational-legal
   d. none of the above

4.   Mahatma Gandhi never held political office in India, but he led that nation's struggle against British colonial control and he is widely regarded as the "father" of modern India. Which type of authority did Gandhi exercise?

    a.   traditional
    b.   rational-legal
    c.   charismatic
    d.   religious

5.   The development of separate and distinct political institutions can be traced to the emergence of:

    a.   horticultural societies
    b.   pastoral groups
    c.   industrial societies
    d.   large-scale agrarian states about 3,000 years ago

6.   In Sweden, most businesses are privately owned, but the government protects workers, provides a number of social services, and tax policies are designed to reduce economic inequality.   This exemplifies a _____ state.

    a.   minimal
    b.   welfare
    c.   sovereign
    d.   none of the above

7.   The political system of the United States emphasizes four main points. Which of the following is NOT one of these?

    a.   the importance of the individual
    b.   consent of the governed
    c.   sponsored mobility
    d.   majority rule and minority rights

8.   Party politics in the United States is shaped by the fact that our political system is a/an _____ democracy.

    a.   absolute
    b.   presidential
    c.   parliamentary
    d.   benevolent

9. In the 1996 presidential election (Clinton vs. Dole), _____
    percent of eligible voters went to the polls.
    a.   48.8
    b.   58.8
    c.   68.8
    d.   78.8

10. As a general rule, which of the following groups is most likely to exercise
    their political rights?
    a.   white, affluent, college-educated Americans
    b.   middle-class workers
    c.   members of racial minorities
    d.   the poor

11. Which of the following best fits the definition of an *interest group*?
    a.   the Congress of the United States
    b.   the United States Senate
    c.   the National Rifle Association
    d.   a university's Board of Trustees

12. The term "lobbies" comes from:
    a.   the fact that all Federal buildings are required to have lobbies
    b.   the old practice of cornering officials in the lobbies of
         government buildings to plead a case
    c.   the tendency for politicians to gravitate toward the lobbies of
         buildings
    d.   the fact that all political legislation is actually voted on in the
         lobby of the House and the Senate

13. Interest groups derive power from which two main sources?
    a.   information and money
    b.   political allegiance and public support
    c.   money and political allegiance
    d.   money and public support

14. The difference between protest movements and PACS is that protest movements:
   a. challenge existing policies
   b. mobilize previously uncommitted citizens
   c. raise funds for a candidate or cause
   d. employ civil disobedience to further their goals

15. Americans who have demonstrated to alert the public to the AIDS epidemic are best described as a/an:
   a. political party
   b. interest group
   c. protest movement
   d. strategic elite

16. In some cases, such as health care reform, opposing and cross-cutting interests lead to inaction. This reflects:
   a. the pluralist view
   b. the power elite view
   c. synthesis
   d. the evolutionary view

17. Who advanced the *power elite* perspective?
   a. David Riesman
   b. Talcott Parsons
   c. C. Wright Mills
   d. G. William Domhoff

18. According to G. William Domhoff, power resides in the hands of:
   a. a small clique who occupy positions of authority
   b. pluralistic interest groups
   c. a national upper class
   d. the power elite

19.   The perspective that agrees that power is concentrated in the hands of a
       few, but argues that they in turn are constrained by the need to satisfy the
       demands of our capitalist economy is the _____ view.
       a.   instrumentalist
       b.   power elite
       c.   pluralist
       d.   structuralist

20.   Which of the following is NOT a type of *authoritarian* political system?
       a.   direct democracy
       b.   dictatorship
       c.   totalitarianism
       d.   monarchy

Answers

1.   b: A government requiring its citizens to pay income taxes and
            Congress voting to commit a nation to war are both examples of
            authority. (Power vs. Authority; p. 517)

2.   d: In our economic system, an employer has the legitimate right to
            hire and fire employees (unless there is a union contract or the
            decision is based on discrimination). (Power and Authority; pp.
            517-518)

3.   a: Traditional authority is based on customs handed down through
            the generations; it is the sacred right of a king, queen, emperor,
            or tribal chief to command his/her subjects. (Power vs.
            Authority; p. 519)

4.   c: Like other charismatic leaders, from Jesus to Mao, Gandhi was
            regarded as a magnetic, powerful leader by his followers. (Power
            and Authority; p. 519)

5.   d: The development of separate and distinct political institutions
            can be traced to the emergence of large-scale agrarian states about
            3,000 years ago.(The Development of Political Institutions; pp.
            520-521)

6.   b: Most Western European countries, including Sweden, are social
            democracies in which the welfare state ideology prevails. (The
            Modern State; p. 523)

7. c: America's political system emphasizes the importance of the individual, consent of the governed, majority rule and minority rights, and equality of opportunity. In a system where sponsored mobility prevails (England, for example), some people, most notably the members of elite families, are singled out for advancement. (Politics in the United States; pp. 523-525)

8. b: If we were an "absolute" democracy, all citizens would actively participate in all decision making; in a parliamentary democracy, people do not vote directly for the head of state; although some may think of our system of government as "benevolent," the correct answer is "presidential democracy." (Party Politics; p. 527)

9. a: In 1996, less than half of eligible voters (48.8 percent) went to the polls. (Politics in America; pp. 526-527)

10. a: Not only are white, affluent, college-educated Americans most likely to exercise their political rights by voting, but they are also more likely to work for a political party or candidate, contribute to campaigns, and participate in community groups, etc. (Electoral Politics: The American Voter; p. 527)

11. c: The Congress of the United States, the United States Senate, and Boards of Trustees are all officially constituted bodies whose members are either elected or appointed to serve a particular institution: the government or a university. The National Rifle Association is one of the most successful and powerful interest groups in this country. (Interest Groups and Political Action Committees; pp. 530-531)

12. b: Interest groups have been part of the American political system from the beginning, but it is doubtful that the framers of the Constitution envisioned lobbying as we know it today. (Interest Groups and Political Action Committees; pp. 530-531)

13. a: Interest groups derive power from information and money. (Interest Groups and Political Action Committees; p. 531)

14. d: All of the other answers apply to both protest movements and PACs. (Interest Groups and Political Action Committees/Protest Movements; pp. 533-535)

15. c: The difference between an interest group and a protest movement is that the former is an organized group designed to promote special interests, and the latter is a grass-roots movement aimed at challenging existing politics and practices. (Protest

Movements; pp. 534-535)

16.   a: Pluralists hold that power in the United States is shared among a multitude of competing interest groups; competition among these interest groups often leads to inaction. (The Pluralist View; pp. 536-537)

17.   c: According to C. Wright Mills, the pluralist view is a romanticized distortion of the truth; most decisions of real importance are made by the power elite. (The Power Elite; p. 536)

18.   c: Domhoff takes the *instrumentalist* perspective, reasoning that members of a national upper class use their wealth to run for public office, sit on corporate boards, or serve in the military. (The Instrumental View; p. 537)

19.   a: According to this view, government must above all maintain a healthy economic order, and it does so by favoring big business and those who control it, whatever their social class. (The Structuralist View; pp. 537-538)

20.   a: A direct democracy is one type of democratic government; monarchies, dictatorships, and totalitarian states are all examples of authoritarian political systems (Types of Political Systems; p. 538)

CRITICAL THINKING

1.   The text points out that authority is legitimate power and that there are several types of authority, including traditional, charismatic, and rational-legal. Consider your own experiences with each type of authority. For example, what type of authority do your parents have over you or do you have over your own children? Have you ever known anyone with charismatic authority? What were the characteristics of this authority?

2.   What are the similarities and differences between authoritarian and democratic political systems? Find examples of each type in the world today. Is there any system that is truly democratic? In what ways is the United States not a true democracy?

WEB EXERCISE: **Touring The White House**

Our government maintains a web site focusing on the executive branch--to wit, the White House:

http://www.whitehouse.gov

This site provides an interesting glimpse at American government, including White House history, facts about the Federal government, news of what is happening on Capitol Hill, and "frequently asked questions" (FAQ's) about the White House.

Go to this site on the Internet and enjoy the ride.

Chapter Fifteen

THE ECONOMY AND WORK

OBJECTIVES

After reading Chapter Fifteen, you should be able to provide detailed answers to the following questions:

1.   What is the global economy and how does it function?
2.   What is capitalism and how does it structure the American economy?
3.   How has the world of work changed? What does work mean to Americans?
4.   How are new technologies changing the nature of work? What effects have they had on people's work satisfaction and leisure time?

CHAPTER REVIEW

I.   **What is the global economy and how does it function?**

Sociologists have argued that the world is no longer composed of separate, individual national economies, as these have been replaced by global corporations. The key actors in today's global economic system are *multinational corporations*: companies with holdings and subsidiaries in several different nations. They tend to perpetuate the global division of labor and the system of stratification that began with European colonization. Multinationals do not compete with other corporations on an equal footing, and they are essentially stateless. The global economy affects American workers directly, because it drains manufacturing jobs into the underdeveloped *Third World* nations of the southern hemisphere, where manufacturing costs are much lower. Third World nations have many problems, however; perhaps the biggest question facing the world today-- and facing the United States as part of the world community--is whether we can find a way to close the gap between the First and Third Worlds.

II.   What is capitalism and how does it structure the American economy?

The economy of the United States is driven by capitalism, which, according to Scottish philosopher Adam Smith, is based on three basic principles: private ownership of property, the profit motive, and free competition. The opposite of a capitalist economy is the *command economy*, found in socialist and communist societies; in a command economy, all or most of the means of production are owned by the state. In reality, no economic system is purely capitalistic or communistic.

The *Industrial Revolution* brought four major technological changes: the harnessing of new sources of power, a more complex division of labor, the birth of the factory, and the use of machines to perform some or all of the tasks previously performed by people. Equally important were advances in *infrastructure* technology.

Today, the United States economy is dominated by *corporations*: business organizations characterized by limited liability, shared ownership (through sale of stocks), and the separation of ownership and management. Who controls corporations internally and to what extent corporations control the economy are matters of intense debate. Among other concerns, the issue of control applies to the role large corporations play in the economy as a whole. *Monopolies*--business firms that control an entire industry--are against the law in the United States. The term for domination of an industry by a small number of large companies is *oligopoly*. A more recent corporate innovation is the *conglomerate*--a company with holdings and subsidiaries in a number of different industries.

The government plays a dual role of enabler and regulator in the economy. Policies based on Keynesian economics, favoring large-scale government intervention to offset depression and inflation, are periodically in and out of favor. As a result of the economic crisis of the 1970s, many policy makers were drawn to two alternative economic theories: monetarism and "supply-side economics."

III.   How has the world of work changed? What is the nature of the work ethic?

Industrialization has had a profound impact on the nature of work. When craftspeople and farmers became factory workers, they lost bargaining power, opportunities for creativity, and control over their own activities, and these trends continue today.

The current shift from an industrial to a service economy has contributed to the development of two separate worlds of work: a primary labor market that offers high wages and promotion opportunities, and a secondary labor market composed of low-skill, low-paying, dead-end jobs.

Despite these trends, the work ethic remains strong, being centered around four themes: maturity is equated with being a good provider; work is seen as the way to freedom and independence; admiration for success; and the feeling that there is built-in dignity in work.

IV.   How has postindustrial social organization changed the nature of work? What effects have the new technologies (computers, etc.) had on people's work satisfaction and leisure time?

Automation (the use of technological control to minimize the need for human workers) is moving from the factory to the office. At the forefront of the U.S. surge toward an *information society* is the computer. Computers and other technologies are creating new opportunities and new challenges in what may be termed a postindustrial society. Computers permit managers to substitute automated machines for people in the factory and to monitor and control the activity of their employees.

The combinations of automation and control seem to be increasing the alienation of workers. Most studies have found that dissatisfaction with work occurs at all occupational levels. In recent decades, full-time employees have experienced a decline in leisure time as the number of working hours has increased.

Daniel Bell has argued that computers and other new technologies are leading toward an *information society* that will be fundamentally different from the industrial society. Other sociologists who agree with this thesis support the functionalist argument that technology itself can alter the shape of society. Critics of this view adopt the conflict view, believing that the impact of technology depends on which groups control its development and use.

CONCEPT REVIEW

Match each of the following terms with the correct definition:

a. monopoly (p. 568)
b. automation (p. 580)
c. infrastructure (p. 564)
d. capitalism (p. 562)
e. service and information economy (p. 575)
f. conglomerate (p. 569)
g. corporation (p. 565)

h. multinational corporation (p. 553)
i. command economy (p. 563)
j. productivity (p. 578)
k. oligopoly (p. 568)
l. Third World (p. 555)
m. alienation (p. 582)
n. dependency theory (p. 560)

1. ___ An economy in which most workers are not directly involved in production.
2. ___ Technological control of production that minimizes the need for human workers.
3. ___ A corporation with holdings and subsidiaries in a number of different industries.
4. ___ The domination of an industry by a small number of large companies.
5. ___ A type of economy characterized by private ownership of property, the profit motive, and free competition.
6. ___ An organization, created by law, whose existence and liabilities are independent of particular owners and managers.
7. ___ The means for moving raw materials, goods, people, and ideas from one place to another in a society or region.
8. ___ The ratio of goods produced to human effort.
9. ___ A firm that controls an entire industry, eliminating competition.
10. ___ An economic system in which the means of production are owned by the state and economic activities are centrally planned.
11. ___ A corporation with holdings and subsidiaries in several different nations.
12. ___ Geographic area comprised of the poorer nations of the southern hemisphere.
13. ___ Suggests that the developing countries have failed to develop the solid modern industrial base and secure middle class that are characteristic of

developed nations because they are economically and politically dependent on foreign corporations.

14.___ The feeling of being separated from one's work and, through one's work, from other people.

Answers

1.	e	6.	g	11.	h
2.	b	7.	c	12.	l
3.	f	8.	j	13.	n
4.	k	9.	a	14.	m
5.	d	10.	i		

REVIEW QUESTIONS

1.   According to the text, the key actors in today's global economic system are:
   a.   independent businesses
   b.   multinational corporations
   c.   socialist organizations
   d.   none of the above

2.   According to the text:
   a.   the first modern multinationals were based in Europe
   b.   multinationals compete with other corporations on an equal footing
   c.   multinationals have alliances with specific "states"
   d.   none of the above

3.   The text points out that the concept of the Third World derives from the old French notion of three estates. Which of the following is NOT one of these?
    a.   the aristocracy
    b.   the Church hierarchy
    c.   the Federales
    d.   the common people (the third estate)

4.   Which of the following does NOT fit with capitalist ideals?
    a.   free and open competition
    b.   centralized planning by the government
    c.   the profit motive
    d.   private ownership of property

5.   According to the text, a *command economy* is:
    a.   the opposite of a capitalist economy
    b.   found in capitalist countries
    c.   the ideal economic organization
    d.   none of the above

6.   According to the text's discussion of multinational corporations:
    a.   the first modern multinationals were based in Europe
    b.   multinationals are essentially "stateless"
    c.   of the fifty largest multinational corporations, about half of them are in the southern hemisphere
    d.   all of the above

7.   A major tire company buys a supermarket chain, timberland, and a movie production company. The company is building a:
    a.   monopoly
    b.   corporation
    c.   conglomerate
    d.   multinational corporation

8.   The description of a corporation as a *person under the law* calls attention to:
       a.   the limited liability of corporations
       b.   the separation of ownership and management
       c.   the diffusion of ownership through the sale of shares
       d.   corporate asymmetry

9.   The text points out that corporations differ from other business organizations in a number of significant ways. Which of the following is NOT one of these?
       a.   limited liability
       b.   separation of ownership and management
       c.   ability to sell shares of ownership
       d.   cannot be sued

10.   Economic competition within the U.S. television industry has led to:
       a.   diversification
       b.   increased quality
       c.   cutbacks and consolidation
       d.   none of the above

11.   Which of the following economists has stressed the role of the government as an enabler for big business?
       a.   Adam Smith
       b.   John Maynard Keynes
       c.   John Galbraith
       d.   Milton Friedman

12.   Which of the following economic theories holds that the government should adopt a laissez-faire posture toward the economy?
       a.   Keynesian economics
       b.   monetarism
       c.   supply-side economics
       d.   trickle-down economics

13.   Which sector of the economy has grown at an accelerated rate in recent years?
        a.   the primary labor market
        b.   the secondary labor market
        c.   information industries
        d.   manufacturing

14.   Today, white-collar work involves:
        a.   only high-prestige, high-paid jobs
        b.   only high-skill jobs
        c.   primarily low-skill jobs
        d.   a mixture of high-paid, low-paid, high-prestige, low-prestige, high -skill, and low-skill jobs

15.   The major difference between a service economy and an industrial economy is that in a service economy:
        a.   automation of the textile and other industries is involved
        b.   government regulation is increased
        c.   a majority of the population is involved in the production of goods
        d.   a majority of the population is *not* involved in the production of goods

16.   Which of the following occupations is NOT in the secondary labor market?
        a.   dishwasher
        b.   janitor
        c.   garment industry worker
        d.   all of the above occupations are part of the secondary labor market

17.   Which of the following is NOT part of the traditional American work ethic?
        a.   standing on one's own two feet
        b.   the belief that work confers dignity
        c.   self-fulfillment
        d.   viewing financial success as a major source of status

18. According to the text, computers:
 a. have increased the ability of organizations to monitor and control resources
 b. enhance individual privacy
 c. challenge the existing distribution of power
 d. none of the above

19. The idea that industrialization dehumanizes work and alienates workers originated with:
 a. Adam Smith
 b. Karl Marx
 c. Emile Durkheim
 d. Richard Edwards

20. According to sociologist Daniel Bell, in "the information society":
 a. technical efficiency will lead to a more rational and humane society
 b. new technologies will continue to automate and manage the production of goods rather than being applied to social planning
 c. people's material needs will take precedence over attention to "higher goods"
 d. none of the above

Answers

1. b: Multinational corporations are companies with holdings and subsidiaries in several different nations, organizing human, natural, and technological resources all over the globe into single economic units. (Multinational Corporations; p. 553)

2. d: The first modern multinationals were based in the United States; they do not compete with other corporations on a equal footing; and they are essentially "stateless." (Multinational Corporations; pp. 553-555)

3. c: The old French notion of three estates consisted of the aristocracy, the Church hierarchy, and the common people (the third estate). (The Economic Crisis in the Third World; p. 555)

4. b: According to capitalist ideology, central planning interferes with

the laws of supply and demand. (Capitalist Ideals; pp. 562-563)

5.   a: In a command economy, all or most of the means of production are owned by the state; economic activities are centrally planned. (Capitalist Ideals; p. 563)

6.   b: Multinationls are essentially "stateless"; the first modern multinationals were based in the United States; of the fifty largest multinational corporations, all are in the northern hemisphere. (Multinational Corporations; pp. 553-555)

7.   c: The term *conglomerate* refers to a large corporation with investments in a number of different industries. In recent years, corporate growth has been due more to diversification than to expansion. (Corporate Capitalism; p. 569)

8.   a: One of the reasons why relatively small companies incorporate is to protect the owners from personal liability. If a corporation becomes bankrupt, its factories and inventory may be sold to pay off debts, but the owner's house and car are *safe*. (Corporate Capitalism; p. 565)

9.   d: Corporations have limited liability; they can sell shares of ownership on the stock market; and ownership and management are separated. Although they have limited liability, corporations can be litigated against. (Corporate Capitalism; pp. 565-566)

10.   c: Television, like any other business, makes changes designed to achieve the maximum amount of profit. Increased competition among the major TV networks has led them to implement budget cutbacks rather than improve their quality to attract more viewers. (Sociology in the Media: Television as Big Business; pp. 570-572)

11.   c: Galbraith was one of the first economists to oppose the conventional wisdom that government is the enemy of big business, by pointing out the role of government as an enabler. (Government and the Economy: Issues and Policies; p. 572)

12.   b: The leading exponent of monetarism in the United States is Milton Friedman, who argues that the government should ensure a stable currency, but otherwise adopt a "hands-off" policy toward the economy; supply-side economics is associated with political figures and its main idea is that Keynesian economics put too much emphasis on consumer demand; the so-called "trickle-down" economic ideology claims that economic prosperity in the

upper reaches of the economy will eventually benefit all members of the society. (Government and the Economy: Issues and Policies; p. 573)

13. b: The shift from an industrial to a service economy is sometimes interpreted as increasing the need for highly skilled *intellectual* workers; in fact, the greatest increase has been in low-skill, low-paying jobs. (The Social Organization of Work; p. 576)

14. d: White-collar work today is different than in the past; it now consists of a variety of salary, prestige, and skill levels. Even the more professional white-collar jobs require less training and offer fewer opportunities for advancement. (The Social Organization of Work; p. 575)

15. d: The term *service* is used loosely to describe any work not directly related to the production of goods, from the job of janitor to that of financial analyst. (The Social Organization of Work; p. 575)

16. d: "Dishwasher," "janitor," and "garment industry worker" all fit the definition of occupations within the secondary labor market: Each is characterized by limited opportunities for advancement, long-time lapses between evaluations and job moves, unchallenging tasks, and few opportunities to master new skills. (What Work Do People Do?; pp. 575-577)

17. c: The idea that leading an independent, creative, and satisfying life is as important as supporting one's family, holding a steady job, or getting ahead is one of the *new rules* that emerged from the counterculture of the 1960s. (The American Work Ethic; p. 578)

18. a: Computers actually increase the opportunities for social control, thus threatening individual privacy. (The Computer Revolution; pp. 579-580)

19. b : Karl Marx predicted that workers in capitalist, industrial societies would become alienated from their work for two primary reasons: First, they would work and sell their labor to someone else rather than for their own gain, and second, they would produce only parts of a product and not the finished goods. (The Impact on Workers; p. 582)

20. a: In "the information society," Bell predicted that technical efficiency will lead to a more rational and human society; technologies that were once used to automate and manage the production of goods will be applied to social planning; and

people's material needs will be met, even beyond the basic level, freeing them to turn their attention to "higher goods." ("The Information Society"; p. 585)

CRITICAL THINKING

1. It has often been said that our capitalist economy is moving in the direction of socialism. What are some of the indications that this trend is occurring? Is this a problem for the United States? Are the many criticisms of command economies justified, or do they merely reflect a tone of ethnocentrism?

2. Daniel Bell's vision of the information society is optimistic about the future, yet other observers are considerably more skeptical. Review the descriptions of the American economy in this chapter. Read the economic/business section of your local newspaper for the next couple of weeks. Do you think that Bell's optimism is justified, or do you agree with his detractors?

WEB EXERCISE: Comparing Economic Philosophies

The text includes an interesting discussion of different economic philosophies: Keynesian, monetarism, and supply-side. The following sites provide some additional information on these issues and by exploring them, you will be able to learn more about these points of view. In addition, you may wish to utilize one of the search engines on the Internet, using the following key words: Keynes, monetarism, supply-side economics.

http://www.oppapers.com/social/ssvskey.txt

http://rs7.loc.gov/lexico/liv/s/supply-side_economics.html

http://econ161.berkeley.edu/politics/Kristol_interesting.html

PART FIVE

THE CHANGING SHAPE OF SOCIETY

Chapter Sixteen

POPULATION, GLOBAL ECOLOGY, AND URBANIZATION

OBJECTIVES

After reading Chapter Sixteen, you should be able to provide detailed answers to the following questions:

1. What are the stages of population growth in industrialized nations? How is this growth pattern different in Third World nations?
2. What are the two major trends concerning population development in the United States?
3. How is the relationship between population and world resources affected by disparities in distribution and consumption? by environmental hazards?
4. How did urbanization affect societies according to nineteenth-century critics like Tonnies, Durkheim, and Marx?
5. What are the three major stages of urbanization in the United States?
6. What are the primary differences between urbanization in rich industrialized nations and in developing countries?

CHAPTER REVIEW

I. What are the stages of population growth in industrialized nations? How is this growth pattern different in Third World nations?

Every second, world population increases by 2.9 persons; estimates are that this population may total as much as 10.7 billion people by the year 2030. The question looms: will the world be able to support this growing population?

The scientific study of population is known as *demography*. Population and population growth rates are highest in Third World nations and lower in western nations. The term *demographic transition* refers to a pattern of major population changes that accompanied the transformation of western nations from agricultural into industrial societies. Western nations have completed this transition. The term refers to a pattern of three distinct stages in population growth. In Stage I, birthrates are high, but death rates are also high, and population growth is slow. In Stage II, birthrates remain high, but death rates decline because of improved agricultural technology, transportation, sanitation, and other related factors. Population growth soars. In Stage III, birthrates decline, and the balance between births and deaths is (slowly) restored.

Most Third World nations are in Stage II of the demographic transition: Death rates have fallen, but birthrates remain high. Because the populations of these countries are young, population growth has a built-in *momentum factor*. Even if couples limit themselves to one or two children, it will be decades before *zero population growth* is achieved. Although there is no simple solution to the problem of population growth in the Third World, analysis of the demographic transition in western nations suggests that economic development is *the best contraceptive*. When people enjoy a high standard of living and social security, they are more likely to limit family size. Raising the status of women has also been linked to smaller families.

II. What are the two major trends concerning population development in the United States?

The fact that a nation like the United States is in Stage III of the demographic transition does not mean that there are no changes in its population profile. The major change in the population of the United States has been a decline in fertility/family size. Americans have fewer children today than they did twenty-five to fifty years ago. One reason for this is the increased availability and use of contraceptives in American society. Another element in this change pattern is a trend among women to postpone marriage and childbirth while they pursue a career or a higher level of education. At present, the overall fertility rate in the United States is one of the lowest in the world. Whether this pattern will continue is difficult to say: Economic conditions may have delayed effects on attitudes.

The second major trend is the changing age structure: The median age of the U.S. population is constantly rising. The American population is "graying." The median age rose from 20 in 1970 to 33 in 1991, and will probably reach 37 by the year 2000. By the year 2030, almost 25 percent of the United States' population will be 65 or older. The graying of America has social as well as economic implications. Older people in the United States, and in many other industrialized nations, do not have the status accorded them in more traditional societies. This lower status is reflected in *ageism*.

III. How is the relationship between population and world resources affected by disparities in distribution and consumption? by environmental hazards?

In the late eighteenth century, Thomas Malthus argued that humanity is condemned to cycles of feast and famine. When food supplies are abundant, the population will grow until, eventually, it outstrips available resources, leading to hunger and war. Was Malthus correct? The text considers two views of the future, analyzes current patterns of supply and distribution, examines technological solutions to short supplies, and then summarizes the current state of affairs.

A. Predicting the future is not a simple matter of arithmetic. Social patterns of supply, distribution, and consumption must also be taken into account. Knowing how many people will be on the earth in the year 2000, how many bushels of wheat will be produced, how many barrels of oil will be available, and the like, does not tell us how many people will be hungry or cold or unemployed. Worldwide food production has increased dramatically within the past two decades. Enough food is produced now to feed 6 billion people, 1 billion more than currently exist on earth. The hunger in the world today is the result of distribution, not supply. The commercialization of agriculture has undermined food self-sufficiency in much of the Third World. Energy shortages are also the result of *distribution, not supply*.

B. Technology produces "miracles," but it also entails environmental risks. The *Green Revolution*, for example, greatly expanded the amount of food produced per acre. But it also increased vulnerability and displaced agricultural workers. The increased food production brought about by the Green Revolution has resulted in lower grain prices, causing Third World nations to go further and further into debt. The problems of production and displacement related to the Green Revolution are further aggravated by overpopulation, which has reduced the amount of available land and deteriorated that land which is available.

C. One of the major problems facing the world today is its consumption patterns. Overpopulation alone is not the critical issue, but the impact of people on ecosystems and nonrenewable resources is a major problem. Consumption patterns for food and fuel are grossly disproportionate, so that industrial nations, especially the United States, are much more extravagant in their use of natural resources. Future supplies of fuel and food are dependent on current patterns of consumption. Continued population growth means that the absolute amounts of energy and fuel needed will continue to increase. In this regard, the depletion of one major renewable resource--trees--needs to be corrected, presumably, by the use of reforestation programs. In the meantime, oil, gas, coal, etc., are NOT renewable. This will not be an easy problem to fix.

D. Environmental risks are also becoming more prevalent in the world today. Oil spills, nuclear power accidents, and air pollution are the most significant threats, but soil pollution is also a problem.

E. Unknown a generation ago, acquired immune deficiency syndrome (AIDS) is today ravaging every continent. This modern plague has the potential to sharply alter world population. Because the epidemic is spreading at an alarming rate, the World Health Organization estimates that 30 to 40 million people will be HIV-positive by the year 2000.

IV.   How did urbanization affect societies according to nineteenth-century critics like Tonnies, Durkheim, and Marx?

Tonnies and Durkheim saw urbanization as destroying traditional communities and creating, instead, interdependence and alienation. For Marx, rural-urban conflict pitted a dying feudalism against a triumphant capitalism, a struggle that in his estimation would produce radical class consciousness and the eventual proletarian revolution.

V.   What are the three major stages of urbanization in the United States?

The urbanization of the United States can be divided into three stages: the emergence of big cities (compact centers of manufacturing and population that developed as a result of industrialization and immigration); the growth of metropolitan regions (geographic expansion made possible by new technologies of transportation and communication, exemplified by the suburban shopping mall); and deconcentration (recent population shifts from the Snow Belt to the Sun Belt and from metropolitan to rural areas). Deconcentration has changed the function and demographics of older cities: Once the centers of manufacturing and affluence in the nation, these cities are now centers for specialized services and warehouses for large segments of the nation's poor.

VI.   What are the primary differences between urbanization in rich industrialized nations and in Third-World countries?

Urbanization in developed countries is tending toward deconcentration, but in the Third World, *megacities* are becoming the rule, because only in these giant urban centers are there adequate transportation and communication facilities, and thus the employment opportunities offered by commerce, industry, and government.

CONCEPT REVIEW

Match each of the following terms with the correct definition:

a. census (p. 600)
b. demographic transition (p. 596)
c. fertility rate (pp. 594-595)
d. life expectancy (p. 595)
e. net growth rate (p. 595
f. zero population growth (p. 597)
g. urbanization (p. 614)
h. momentum factor (p. 597)
i. invasion and succession (p. 618)

j. birthrate (p. 594)
k. death rate (p. 594)
l. demography (p. 594)
m. megacity (p. 621)
n. ageism (p. 603)
o. mechanical solidarity (p. 615)
p. gemeinschaft (p. 615)
q. organic solidarity (p. 615)
r. gessellschaft (p. 615)

1.___ The number of births per 1,000 people in a population in a given year.
2.___ The percentage increase in a population, in a given period, taking into account immigration and emigration as well as birth and death rates.
3.___ The scientific study of population.
4.___ Population growth that will occur because a large percentage of the population is in or about to enter its childbearing years.
5.___ A systematic count of an entire population taken every ten years.
6.___ A pattern of major population changes that accompanied the transformation of western nations from agricultural into industrial societies.
7.___ The number of deaths per 1,000 people in a population in a given year.
8.___ The potential life span of the average individual in a given population.
9.___ The number of live births per 1,000 women of childbearing age (fifteen to forty-four) in a population in a given year.
10.___ The point where birth and death rates are equal, so that the population is stable.
11.___ The ecological process whereby the members of one racial, ethnic, or socioeconomic group will begin to move into an area and as their numbers build up, they will eventually "succeed" the group previously living there, replacing it as the dominant group in the neighborhood or in the entire city.
12.___ An increase in the percentage of a population living in urban settlements

and a resulting extension of the influence of urban culture and life styles.

13.___ A city with a population of 10 million or more.

14.___ Subtle and not so subtle forms of prejudice and discrimination against older people.

15.___ A sense of belonging and community, reflected in shared norms and values, frequent social contact, and warm personal relationships.

16.___ A type of social organization based on similarity that is typical in traditional societies.

17.___ A type of social organization based on interdependence that is typical in modern, industrial societies.

18.___ A type of social order that is characterized by association, wherein change is constant, there is little consensus on values and norms, and social contacts are fleeting and impersonal.

Answers

1.	j	7.	k	13.	m
2.	e	8.	d	14.	n
3.	l	9.	c	15.	p
4.	h	10.	f	16.	o
5.	a	11.	i	17.	q
6.	b	12.	g	18.	r

REVIEW QUESTIONS

1. The human population of the earth presently stands at a little over 5 billion. Estimates are that by the year 2030, it may reach:
   a. 6.3 billion
   b. 8 billion
   c. 10.7 billion
   d. over 20 billion

2.   Unlike most other demographic measures, population growth rates are calculated:
   a.   as percentages
   b.   numerically
   c.   using family size as the primary indicator
   d.   only in terms of fertility rate

3.   A nation enters Stage III of the demographic transition when birth- rates decline to replacement levels and the population growth rate slows down. Which of the following has helped to slow population growth in Western nations?
   a.   economic development
   b.   modern birth-control methods
   c.   Social Security programs
   d.   all of the above

4.   Changes in population growth patterns in developing nations differ from those that occurred in western nations in that:
   a.   in the developing nations, unlike western nations, death rates have fallen but birthrates remain high
   b.   the decline in death rates in developing nations is due in large part to imported technology, medicine, and food.
   c.   changes that took several hundred years in western nations have occurred in a matter of decades in developing nations
   d.   all of the above

5.   An elderly gentleman from India observes that the biggest change in his lifetime is that: "We have learned how to keep from dying." This observation illustrates that India is in which stage of the demographic transition?
   a.   Stage I
   b.   Stage II
   c.   Stage III
   d.   This observation does not apply to the demographic transition.

6.   The most successful large-scale effort to limit population has been taking place in:
   a.   the United States
   b.   Great Britain
   c.   France
   d.   China

7.   According to the text, which of the following are the two major changes in the population of the United States?
   a.   declining fertility and declining mortality
   b.   changing age structure and declining mortality
   c.   declining fertility and changing age structure
   d.   the demographic transition and migration

8.   Which of the following social phenomena is NOT a result of the demographic episode known as the baby boom?
   a.   the growth of child-centered industries in the 1950s and 1960s
   b.   the oversupply of schools and teachers in the late 1970s
   c.   the under supply of men of marriageable age in the 1960s and 1970s
   d.   the growth of the retirement industry

9.   At the time of his writings in the late 1700s, Thomas Malthus did not anticipate:
   a.   improvements in agricultural productivity
   b.   widespread use of birth control
   c.   changing attitudes toward family size
   d.   all of the above

10.   The problem of world hunger is primarily one of food:
   a.   production
   b.   distribution
   c.   consumption
   d.   preservation

11.   Worldwide, consumption of food and other patterns of consumption are:
      a.   extremely lopsided
      b.   fairly equal
      c.   distributed evenly
      d.   b and c above

12.   Which of the following may be a result of the greenhouse effect?
      a.   Polar ice caps would melt.
      b.   Sea level would rise.
      c.   Land would become arid and unusable
      d.   all of the above

13.   Allan Schnaiberg argues that once set in motion, industrialized production develops a momentum of its own. He calls this the:
      a.   Green Revolution
      b.   greenhouse effect
      c.   momentum factor
      d.   none of the above

14.   According to the World Health Organization, by the year 2000, _____ million people will be HIV-positive.
      a.   10
      b.   30-40
      c.   100
      d.   200

15.   Which functionalist sociologist referred to the modern, industrial social order as *gesellshaft*?
      a.   Emile Durkheim
      b.   Herbert Gans
      c.   Ferdinand Tonnies
      d.   Karl Marx

16.   Durkheim reasoned that:
      a.   traditional societies are based on organic solidarity
      b.   modern, industrial societies are based on mechanical solidarity
      c.   organic solidarity is based on interdependence
      d.   all of the above

17.   Where Tonnies and Durkheim were concerned with social cohesion, Karl Marx was interested in:
   a.   the sources of social conflict
   b.   organic solidarity
   c.   mechanical solidarity
   d.   none of the above

18.   The urban history of the United States can be divided into three stages. Which of the following is NOT one of these?
   a.   emergence of small towns
   b.   growth of metropolitan regions
   c.   suburbanization
   d.   none of the above

19.   In the 1920s, a group of sociologists at the University of Chicago, led by Robert Park, began investigating urban changes by treating the city as:
   a.   a gesellschaft
   b.   a gemeinschaft
   c.   a kind of social organism/an ecosystem
   d.   none of the above

20.   According to the text, urban growth in the Third World is different from urban growth in rich industrial nations in which of the following ways?
   a.   In Third World countries, transportation and communications are well developed.
   b.   The governments of most Third World nations have powerful control over the countryside.
   c.   In most Third World cities, the formal sector is a central source of livelihood for large numbers of recent migrants.
   d.   none of the above

Answers

1. c: Every second, world population increases by 2.9 persons; a population of just 2 billion people is equal to the entire population of the world in 1930, or almost 1,000 times the population of the United States today. (Introduction; p. 594)

2. a: Suppose a nation has a birthrate of 28 (per 1,000), a death rate of 17, and little immigration or emigration. Its population is increasing at the rate of 11 per 1000 (28 minus 17); its growth rate is 1.1 percent. (Demography: The Study of Population; p. 595)

3. d: Economic development, modern birth-control methods, and Social Security programs were all mentioned as possible variables that have helped to slow population growth in the Western nations. (World Patterns; p. 597)

4. d: Western nations did go through a period when death rates fell but birthrates remained high; in the West, this stage was followed by a period of industrial expansion and economic growth. In the Third World, economic growth is not catching up with population growth. (World Patterns; p. 597)

5. b: The population explosion in Stage II of the demographic transition is due more to a decline in death rates than to an increase in birthrates. (World Patterns; pp. 596-597)

6. d: In China, government-mandated family planning has been in place for nearly three decades. (Population Growth in Developing Nations; p. 598)

7. c: The two major changes are declining fertility and the changing age structure. The major change in the population of the United States has been a decline in family size; the second reason for low fertility rates in this country is that women are postponing marriage and childbirth. (The Population of the United States; p. 600)

8. d: The baby boom generation is now in its thirties and forties and has yet to reach retirement age. The growth of the retirement industry is due to increases in longevity, not the baby boom. All of the other answers describe changes resulting from the large difference in generation size. (The Population of the United States; pp. 601-602)

9. d: Malthus did not foresee the impact of scientific technology on

agricultural productivity nor did he anticipate that people could or would reduce family size through birth control procedures. (Population and Global Ecology; pp. 603; 605)

10.   b: Worldwide food production has increased dramatically, and even though consumption patterns are unequal, distribution is the underlying issue in world hunger. (Food Supplies and Distribution; p. 605)

11.   a: With only about 25 percent of the world's population, industrial nations consume nearly 80 percent of its energy resources; people in industrial nations not only have more to eat than those in developing nations, but also eat better quality food. (Patterns of Consumption; p. 607)

12.   d.   The greenhouse effect results from a buildup of gases in the atmosphere which allows heat to enter the atmosphere but not to escape. This increases the temperature of the earth over time, causing land to become arid and sea level to rise. (Environmental Risks; pp. 609-610)

13.   d: Schnaiberg believes that the rich nations are caught on a "treadmill of production," wherein people are replaced by machines, energy use accelerates, and higher levels of pollution result. (Environmental Risks; p. 612)

14.   b: By 1993 in the United States, an estimated 1 million were infected and about 195,000 had died; because the epidemic is spreading at an alarming rate, the World Health Organization estimates that 30 to 40 million people will be HIV positive by the year 2000. (AIDS and Population; p. 613)

15.   c: Functionalist sociologists saw industrialization and urbanization as destroying traditional communities and primary groups, thus setting the individual adrift. People do not feel they belong to a city; they merely use its resources. (Urbanization and Sociology; p. 615)

16.   c: Traditional societies are based on mechanical solidarity; modern societies are based on organic solidarity; whereas mechanical solidarity is based on similarity, organic solidarity is based on interdependence. (Urbanization and Sociology; p. 615)

17.   a: Marx was interested in the sources of social conflict; he saw the division between town and country in the nineteenth century as

reflecting an underlying conflict between two competing modes of production. (Urbanization and Sociology; p. 615)

18.   a: The three stages are: the emergence of big cities, the growth of metropolitan regions, and suburbanization. (The Urbanization of the United States; pp. 616-618)

19.   c: Park and his colleagues borrowed concepts from biology and viewed the city as being composed of specialized, interdependent parts. (Urban Ecology; p. 618)

20.   d: None of these characteristics is typical of Third World nations. (Urbanization in Global Perspective; pp. 621-622)

CRITICAL THINKING

1.   Population and environment are closely interrelated social problems: Population issues directly affect the environment and environmental concerns have a direct impact on population. Discuss this delicate relationship, paying special attention to the concept of the ecosystem.

2.   Most people in the United States live in urban or suburban areas. On a continuum running from the rural to the urban, where would the community in which your school is located fall? If this community differs from your hometown, explain how it is different.

WEB EXERCISE: Exploring the United States Census Bureau

The text briefly discusses the United States *census*, pointing out that this is the primary source of information concerning a wide variety of statistical facts about the nation's population. The U.S. government has a web site that will allow you to explore many different aspects of the demography of this country:

http://www.census.gov/

Chapter Seventeen

COLLECTIVE BEHAVIOR AND SOCIAL MOVEMENTS

OBJECTIVES

After reading Chapter Seventeen, you should be able to provide detailed answers to the following questions:

1. Ranging from fads to riots, is collective behavior rational or irrational behavior?
2. What explanations exist for riots? What caused the Los Angeles riot of 1992, and how does this disturbance compare with the urban riots of the 1960s?
3. How does a social movement differ from other forms of collective behavior? What explains the success or failure of a social movement?
4. How is a social revolution distinguished from other types of social movements? Are social revolutions rational or irrational behavior?

CHAPTER REVIEW

I. **Ranging from fads to riots, is collective behavior rational or irrational behavior?**

Collective behavior involves large numbers of people engaging in nonroutine activities that violate social expectations.

Among sociologists, there are two different ways of viewing mass departures from social expectations and normative behavior.

The first view, especially common among *functionalists*, interprets collective behavior as a symptom that something has gone "haywire" in the social system; functionalists emphasize the spontaneous and emotional aspects of *all* collective behavior.

For many years, the functionalist view dominated the study of collective behavior. In recent years, however, a new approach--rooted in conflict theory--has taken shape. *Collective action theory* sees most, if not all, collective behavior as the result of rational decisions on the part of individuals, and planning and organization on the part of collectives. Collective action theorists emphasize the real grievances, rational choices, and organization underlying social movements and revolutions, which they distinguish from sudden, short-lived outbreaks of unconventional behavior, such as fads, crazes, and hysterias.

II.   What explanations exist for riots? What caused the Los Angeles riot of 1992, and how does this disturbance compare with the urban riots of the 1960s?

Functionalists and symbolic interactionists see riots as a breakdown in social order and emphasize the irrational, chaotic, and destructive aspects of riots. Conflict theorists and collective action theorists see most riots as challenges to the existing social order based on real grievances and emphasize the selective, goal-oriented aspects of crowd violence. *Crowd* is a neutral term that refers to a collection of people who come together on a temporary basis. *Mob* is a loaded term that refers to a "disorderly, riotous, or lawless crowd of people."

The 1992 Los Angeles riot was precipitated by a collective sense of outrage at police brutality and what was perceived as a gross miscarriage of justice, but its intensity was fueled by the relative deprivation felt by South Central Los Angeles residents when they compared themselves with successful immigrants and more upwardly mobile families. In contrast, the urban riots of the 1960s took place at a time when minorities had come to expect a better life, but their expectations were not being met.

There are a number of microperspectives concerning crowd violence. Some sociologists argue that crowd violence can be explained through crowd psychology. Gustav LeBon supported a contagion theory of crowd behavior. Years later, Herbert Blumer updated LeBon's description of crowds. Not all crowds are violent. *Expressive crowds* gather to express a common emotion. Ralph Turner and Lewis Killian reject the notion that crowds are normless, arguing instead that crowd behavior reflects the development of new or *emergent norms*. Using collective action theory, Richard Berk argued that far from being irrational, behavior in crowds is determined by rational calculation.

There are a number of macroperspectives concerning crowd violence. James Davies argues that *rising expectations* play a role in many, if not most, outbreaks of civil disorder. Davies reasons that severe poverty and extreme powerlessness lead to apathy and hopelessness. Another important factor in the Los Angeles riot was *relative deprivation*: Whether people feel deprived depends in large part on the groups to which they compare themselves.

Collective behavior can be seen as a breakdown in social order. When the contagious element in collective madness is fear or anxiety rather than anger and frustration, the result is *mass hysteria*. When the contagion involves wild enthusiasm about some person, object, or activity, the result is called a *craze*.

The text uses the Branch Davidians, the Oklahoma City bombing incident, and the militia movement in the United States as examples in illustrating sociologist Neil Smelser's functional theory. Smelser has argued that for any episode of collective behavior to occur, a number of preconditions must be met. Smelser's functional theory of collective behavior holds that for discontent to be translated into collective action, six conditions must be met. (1) Structural Conduciveness: the social structure must create uncertainty and channels for communication of discontent; (2) Structural Strain: people must feel that things are getting out of control; (3) Generalized Belief: people must develop shared ideas about what is threatening them and how to respond; (4) Precipitating Incident: something must happen to confirm people's suspicions; (5) Mobilization: someone (or some group) must take charge, providing direction; (6) Breakdown of Social Control: even if the first five conditions have been met, collective behavior will not occur if conventional sources of social control (from the family to the police) intervene.

III.   **How does a social movement differ from other forms of collective behavior? What explains the success or failure of a social movement?**

A *social movement* is the organized effort of a large number of people to produce some social change. Social movements differ from collective behavior in three ways: they are longer-lasting, more purposeful and goal-oriented, and more structured. A social movement depends on the participation of a core of active members. People who benefit from a movement but who do not participate in it are known as *free riders*. Functionalists view collective behavior as a breakdown in social order fueled by generalized, often irrational beliefs and fired by a precipitating and usually ambiguous incident. Collective action theorists begin with the assumption that the struggle over power is a universal feature of social life- - an assumption they share with more general conflict theories. Charles Tilly's theory of collective action illustrates this perspective and holds that collective action is part of the normal fabric of everyday life. Small-scale or not, localized collective action which becomes a full-scale social movement depends on interests (people developing a sense of common purpose), organization (informal, preexisting groups and networks may lay the groundwork and formal organizations develop later on), mobilization of resources, and opportunity. Though not included in Tilly's list of factors, the media are also an element of social movements. In some cases, social movements result in social change, but in others they may delay change by scoring only symbolic victories or by mobilizing opposition. A group which is well organized, which mobilizes its resources effectively, and which is strengthened by rising expectations is likely to meet with success.

There are a variety of theories of social movements. Early theories focused on individual personalities and the grievances of social movement participants. Relative deprivation is one example of these early theories. Two other early theories also focused on the individual: the *personality theory* and *mass society theory*.

Those who attribute social movements to a breakdown in social order also tend to portray social movements as a departure from routine, rational, everyday behavior. Those who attribute social movements to the creation of new social structures tend to analyze the life cycle of social movements, from "birth to death." Contemporary collective action theorists see social movements as the rational extension, or intensification, of the struggles for power that go on every day in every society and have no clear beginning or end. The term *collective action frames* refers to a mechanism through which individuals may understand what happens around them, come to identify the sources of their problems, and devise ways to address their grievances. Current research on social movements is also concerned with the concept of "new social movements." This theory attempts to encompass both psychological and structural factors.

The text discusses the disability rights movement as an example of a contemporary social movement. The struggle of the disabled underscores one of the main tenets of collective action theory: Power struggles are a regular feature of social life and are often necessary to produce basic advances in social conditions.

The term "social movement" implies change and the relationship between social movements and social change is complex. Some movements actively resist change. A social movement that is mounted to resist a movement already under way is known as a *countermovement*. Social movements may boomerang in other ways, turning formerly neutral or even sympathetic people into opponents.

Social movements may also open people to new ideas and provide an opportunity for individuals to test their convictions.

IV.   How is a social revolution distinguished from other types of social movements? Are social revolutions rational or irrational behavior?

A *social revolution* goes beyond a social movement in that it involves a rapid, fundamental transformation of a country's political system, social class structure, and dominant ideology. Skocpol challenges the popular view that revolutions are started by small bands of radicals, driven by an ideology and intent on political upheaval. The structure of international relations, especially the threat of invasion, conflicts among powerful groups within the society, and preexisting organizations that facilitate mass uprisings are very important. More often then not, leadership emerges after a revolution has taken place and creates a more centralized, bureaucratic government than existed under the old regime. The ideology or rationalization also develops after a revolution is under way. When revolutions succeed, what once seemed irrational now seems rational; yesterday's rioters become today's heroes. Revolutionary change calls attention to historical biases, which exist in all sociological theories.

CONCEPT REVIEW

Match each of the following terms with the correct definition.

a.	collective behavior (p. 628)	j.	generalized belief (p. 638)
b.	mob (p. 630)	k.	crowd (p. 630)
c.	structural strain (p. 638)	l.	craze (p. 635
d.	precipitating incident (p. 638)	m.	mass society theory (p. 644)
e.	structural conduciveness (p. 638)	n.	mass hysteria (p. 635)
f.	social movement (p 639)	o.	social revolution (p. 650)
g.	breakdown of social control (p. 638)	p.	rising expecta- tions (p. 639)
h.	emergent norms (p. 633)	q.	relative depriva- tion (p. 634)
i.	mobilization (p. 638)	r.	countermovement (p. 649)
		s.	expressive crowds (p. 633)

t.   free riders (p. 640)
u.   personality theory (p. 644)
v.   collective action theory
       (p. 629)

1.____   Smelser's first condition for collective behavior; an element within the structure that invites or drives people to depart from routine behavior.

2.____   A loaded term for crowds that are viewed as disorderly, riotous, or lawless.

3.____   Smelser's third condition for collective behavior; the shared perception among individuals about who or what is threatening them, what the enemy is like, and how they can and should respond.

4.____   The more or less organized effort of a large number of people to produce some social change.

5.____   Smelser's second condition for collective behavior; the tension that develops when people sense an immediate, ambiguous threat and feel helpless to do anything about it.

6.____   The view of collective behavior that emphasizes rational decisions on the part of individuals and planning and organization on the part of collectivities.

7.____   Smelser's fifth condition for collective behavior; the behavior of an official or unofficial leader who suggests a course of action and provides a model for behavior.

8.____   A type of collective behavior that involves wild enthusiasm about some person, object, or activity.

9.____   Smelser's sixth condition for collective behavior; the absence of leadership capable of correcting misinformation, convincing people that the threat is imaginary, or intervening to redirect behavior.

10.____ Large numbers of people engaging in nonroutine activities that violate social expectations.

11.____ Smelser's fourth condition for collective behavior; a dramatic event that confirms people's fears and suspicions and focuses their attention.

12.____ Definitions of the situation during crowd behavior.

13.____ A rapid, fundamental transformation of a country's political system, social-class structure, and dominant ideology.

14.____ A collection of people who come together on a temporary basis.

15.____ Collective behavior that results from the *contagious* spread of fear or anxiety.

16.___ A condition where the gap between what people expect and what they actually have becomes intolerable.

17.___ A social movement that is mounted to resist a movement already under way.

18.___ Feelings of deprivation that are contingent on the groups to which people compare themselves (reference groups).

19.___ Explains participation in social movements as a way to satisfy a person's individual needs rather than to address social grievances, and, therefore, the participant is seen as deviant or personally troubled.

20.___ Crowds that gather to express a common emotion such as joy, excitement, or grief.

21.___ People who benefit from a social movement but do not participate in it.

22.___ The (more or less) organized effort of a large number of people to produce some social change

Answers

1.	e	9.	g	17.	r
2.	b	10.	a	18.	q
3.	j	11.	d	19.	u
4.	f	12.	h	20.	s
5.	c	13.	o	21.	t
6.	m	14.	k	22.	v
7.	i	15.	n		
8.	l	16.	p		

REVIEW QUESTIONS

1. According to the text's discussion of functionalist and collective action theorists:
   a. collective action theorists interpret collective behavior as a symptom that something has "gone haywire" in the social system
   b. historically, collective action theory has dominated the study of collective behavior
   c. functionalists view collective behavior as the result of rational decision making
   d. none of the above

2. According to the text's discussion of "tulipomania" (*A Global View*):
   a. sometime after the year 1636, Dutch citizens stopped buying tulips and rich people became paupers overnight
   b. everyone associates tulips with the United States
   c. the craze for tulips peaked between 1902 and 1920
   d. none of the above

3. Which of the following is not an example of collective behavior?
   a. a wildcat strike
   b. a protest at a nuclear power plant
   c. the St. Patrick's Day parade in New York City
   d. the revolution in Iran

4. The riot that broke out in Los Angeles in 1992 was the first major upheaval in that city since the Watts riot of 1965. The riot broke out after:
   a. the not-guilty verdict in the Rodney King trial
   b. the shooting of an African-American youth by the L.A.P.D.
   c. economic hard times accelerated in the city
   d. harassment of African-Americans on the streets of L.A.

5. Which of the following is a *microlevel* explanation of riots?
   a. relative deprivation
   b. emergent norms
   c. the riffraff theory
   d. the rabble rouser theory

6.　　Which of the following is a *macrolevel* explanation of riots?
　　　a.　　emergent norms
　　　b.　　rational calculation theory
　　　c.　　the global theory
　　　d.　　relative deprivation

7.　　A number of years ago, disaffected members of the Seventh-Day Adventist church set up a communal farm near Waco, Texas. That group also splintered, and one branch came under the leadership of a man named David Koresh. This group became known as the:
　　　a.　　People's Temple
　　　b.　　Branch Davidians
　　　c.　　Moonies
　　　d.　　Farm

8.　　Which of the following is the best illustration of Smelser's fifth condition for collective behavior, *mobilization*?
　　　a.　　Several books describing the aftermath of a nuclear war make the best-seller lists.
　　　b.　　A committee is formed to contact church congregations, heads of student governments, women's groups, environmental groups, and others who might be concerned about the arms race.
　　　c.　　Local officials refuse to grant a permit for a demonstration.
　　　d.　　News media give coverage to antinuclear demonstrations in Europe.

9.　　The FBI's April 19th assault on the Branch Davidian Compound illustrates which of Smelser's preconditions for collective behavior?
　　　a.　　generalized belief
　　　b.　　structural strain
　　　c.　　precipitating incident
　　　d.　　breakdown of social control

10.   One of the criticisms of Smelser's functionalist theory of collective behavior is that it:
    a.   is irrational
    b.   overemphasizes planning and organization
    c.   overstates the differences between collective action and everyday behavior
    d.   underplays emotional factors

11.   Which of the following is NOT one of the elements of collective action theory?
    a.   common interests
    b.   organization
    c.   mobilization of resources
    d.   authoritarian decision making

12.   Which of the following is NOT one of the reasons that the San Francisco demonstration by disabled people succeeded?
    a.   willingness to engage in civil disobedience
    b.   preexisting organization
    c.   resources
    d.   rising expectations

13.   When the women's rights movement seemed close to getting the Equal Rights Amendment passed in the 1970s, Phyllis Schlafly and her supporters successfully blocked passage of the amendment. Schlafly's efforts may be most accurately defined as a:
    a.   social movement
    b.   countermovement
    c.   backlash
    d.   radical reactionary movement

14.   Skocpol emphasizes the role of international forces in social revolutions. She found that revolutions are most likely to take place when:
    a.   foreign agitators introduce a new ideology into a country
    b.   a developed nation's economy begins to falter
    c.   an underdeveloped nation is threatened or attacked by a technologically more advanced nation
    d.   international alliances fall apart

15.   Skocpol identifies four factors that social revolution depends upon. Which of the following is NOT one of these?
       a.   global inequality and international competition
       b.   a clash of interests between the state or government and powerful groups within the society
       c.   popular uprisings
       d.   emergence of a charismatic leader

16.   The "last straw" in terms of the Iranian Revolution was:
       a.   disgust with the Shah's militarism and ties to the United States
       b.   the announcement of plans to close the Teheran bazaar and attacks on the clergy
       c.   the taking of U.S. hostages
       d.   the Shiite tradition of martyrdom

17.   In her book *Backlash: The Undeclared War Against American Women*, Susan Faludi details how the:
       a.   media ignored evidence showing that single women are happy and fulfilled and marry if they choose to
       b.   Equal Rights Amendment failed
       c.   fight for Affirmative Action damaged women more than it assisted them
       d.   none of the above

18.   During the late 1980s and early 1990s, groups of citizens in Pennsylvania mobilized in order to oppose the location in their communities of:
       a.   halfway houses for juvenile offenders
       b.   asylums for mental patients
       c.   waste incinerators
       d.   none of the above

19.   According to the text's summary discussion:
a.   most sociologists view collective action theory as an unnecessary companion to the more practical functionalist explanation
b.   collective action theory overstates the irrationality of collective behavior
c.   functionalist theory tends to underestimate the emotional components of collective behavior
d.   none of the above

20.   One of the criticisms of collective action theory is that it:
a.   is irrational
b.   puts too much emphasis on generalized beliefs
c.   overstates the differences between collective action and everyday behavior
d.   underplays emotional factors

Answers

1.   d.   Functionalists interpret collective behavior as a symptom that something has "gone haywire" in the social system; historically, functionalism has dominated the study of collective behavior; collective action theorists view collective behavior as the result of rational decision making. (Rational or Irrational?; pp. 628-629)

2.   a: Everyone associates tulips with Holland; in that country, the craze for tulips peaked between 1634 and 1636, after which the "mania" ceased. (*A Global View*: "Tulipomania: A Historical Perspective"; p. 636)

3.   c: The St. Patrick's Day parade is a scheduled event, structured by traditional norms and values. The rowdy enthusiasm and occasionally destructive behavior of crowds after the parade does fit the definition, however. (Collective Behavior as a Breakdown in Social Order; p. 628)

4.   a: The 1992 riot was helped along by the televised absence of police in South Central L.A., where the crowd violence began. (The 1992 Los Angeles Riot: A Case Study; p. 632)

5.   b: Microlevel theories focus on interpersonal relations--in this case, how people decide how to behave in an ambiguous situation.

The concept of emergent norms highlights the observation that, even in riots, behavior is not random. (Microperspectives: Crowd Psychology or Collective Action?; p. 633)

6. d: Macroperspectives address the question of *why* riots occur at a particular time and place. Rising expectations and relative deprivation are key elements in the macroperspectives on crowd violence. (Macroperspectives: Rising Expectations and Relative Deprivation; pp. 634-635)

7. b: The leader of the Branch Davidians, David Koresh, saw himself as an agent of God who would be transformed into a warrior angel at the battle that would end the world, and he predicted that the end would take place in Texas. (The Branch Davidians; p. 635)

8. b: According to Smelser, discontent will not be translated into collective behavior unless people are organized. (Smelser's Functionalist View; pp. 638-639)

9. c: A precipitating incident is a dramatic event that confirms people's fears and suspicions; this tips a scale already weighted by structural conduciveness, strain, and a generalized belief. (Smelser's Functionalist View; p. 638)

10. c: Collective action theorists, in particular, argue that the line between everyday conflict and collective behavior is never definite. In their view, a major problem for social scientists is distinguishing what is and what is not collective behavior. (Smelser's Functionalist View/An Evaluation; p. 639)

11. d: The elements of collective action are: common interest, organization, resource mobilization, and opportunity. (Elements of Collective Action; pp. 640-643)

12. a: The text cites three elements in the success of the San Francisco demonstration: preexisting organization, resources, and rising expectations. (Mobilizing the Disabled; p. 647)

13. b: A social movement that is mounted to resist a movement already under way is a *countermovement*. (Social Change; p. 649)

14. c: Skocpol's primary example is the Russian Revolution, which began when Russia was threatened by Germany's military might. (Skocpol's Theory of Social Revolution; p. 652)

15. d: Skocpol's four factors are: global inequality and international competition, a clash of interests between the state or government

and powerful groups within the society, popular uprisings, and the production of a more powerful government than existed under the old regime. (Skocpol's Theory of Social Revolution; p. 652)

16. b: The plan to attack the Teheran bazaar and attacks on the clergy represented the *last straw*; these acts had the unintended consequence of galvanizing support for Islamic rebels among shopkeepers. (The Iranian Revolution; p. 654)

17. a: Faludi's book details how the media ignored evidence showing that single women are happy and fulfilled and marry if they choose to. (*Sociology and the Media*: "Single Women Targeted in the Popular Press"; pp. 644-645)

18. c: These groups of Pennsylvanians mobilized in order to protest the location of waste incinerators in their home communities. (*Closeup*: "Backyards, NIMBYs, and Incinerator Sitings"; pp. 650-651)

19. d: Most sociologists view collective action theory as an important correction of the more conservative functionalist and psychosocial theories of collective behavior and social movements; functionalism has been criticized for overstating the irrationality of collective behavior; collective action theory tends to underestimate the emotional components. (An Evaluation [conclusion]; p. 656)

20. c: Collective action theorists, in particular, argue that the line between everyday conflict and collective behavior is never definite. In their view, a major problem for social scientists is distinguishing what is and what is not collective behavior. (An Evaluation [conclusion]; p. 656)

CRITICAL THINKING

1.   Periodically, the United States has suffered from spasms of violence and disruption. Other than the Los Angeles riot of 1992, the past two decades have been relatively peaceful in this regard. Are there any social conditions (Smelser's "structural strain") existing today in the United States that could produce violent episodes of collective behavior? Describe the conditions and the forms of collective behavior that might result. What conditions would have to exist before YOU might be swept up in a riot or other form of collective behavior?

2.   During the past few decades, the environmental movement has become an important social movement in many industrial societies. How has the environmental movement in the United States affected social change, either by encouraging change or by impeding it? In your judgment, have the effects of the movement been good or bad?

WEB EXERCISE: **Exploring The Militia Movement**

The text discusses the formation of militias as an example of collective behavior and social movements. Since the Oklahoma City bombing incident, there has been increased attention paid to this phenomenon and this exposure is reflected on the Internet and World Wide Web. The following sites provide an excellent overview of the militia movement in American society and also some links to other interesting sites that relate to this type of collective behavior:

http://www.militia-watchdog.org

http://www.igc.apc.org/an/militia.html